SpringerBriefs in Law

More information about this series at http://www.springer.com/series/10164

Charles Foster · Jonathan Herring

Human Thriving and the Law

Springer

Charles Foster
Green Templeton College
University of Oxford
Oxford, UK

Jonathan Herring
Exeter College
University of Oxford
Oxford, UK

ISSN 2192-855X ISSN 2192-8568 (electronic)
SpringerBriefs in Law
ISBN 978-3-030-01134-5 ISBN 978-3-030-01135-2 (eBook)
https://doi.org/10.1007/978-3-030-01135-2

Library of Congress Control Number: 2018955920

This Springer imprint is published by the registered company Springer Nature Switzerland AG
The registered company address is: Gewerbestrasse 11, 6330 Cham, Switzerland

CF: To the memory of Micky Weingarten,
a wise, kind, and iconoclastic friend.

JH: To the memory of Earline Johnson,
my loving mother in law

Preface

The idea of the Good Life—of what constitutes human thriving—is, implicitly, the foundation and justification of the law. The law exists to hold societies together; to hold in tension the rights of individuals as against individuals, the rights of individuals as against various types of non-humans such as corporations (and vice versa), and the rights of individuals as against the state (and vice versa). In democratic states, laws inhibit some freedoms in the name of greater, or more desirable freedoms. The only justification for law is surely that it tends to promote human thriving.

But what is the Good Life? What does it mean to live a thriving life? There has been no want of discussion, at least since the great Athenians. But surprisingly, since human thriving is its sole raison d'être, the law has been slow to contribute to the conversation, or even put snippets of the conversation in its footnotes.

The opinions of the philosophers are now supplemented by a good deal of evidence about what makes humans happy. 'Happiness' may not be the whole story of human thriving, but it is part of it, and some scientific investigations of happiness cast significant light on the ingredients of *eudaemonia*.

This new evidence, like the philosophical discourse, has not yet filtered into the law courts. It cannot be kept out for long. Judges regularly determine whether a particular course of action is in the 'best interests' of a child or an incapacitous adult. Those determinations—which are often quite literally life or death decisions—can and should be informed by all the available evidence.

Best interests determinations are something of a scandal. Every single one of them presumes an account of what it means to thrive. Not one of them sets out explicitly which account is being used. It is like a judge saying that she is going to find for the claimant, but refusing to say under which enactment.

We hope that this book will:

- Make lawyers ask: 'What is the law for?', and conclude that it is to maximise human thriving.
- Make lawyers ask: 'But what does human thriving mean?', and conclude that they need to be anthropologists and philosophers and biologists and poets in order to be proper lawyers, and that instead of reading law books, they should

go back to ancient Athens and wander from there to modern neurobiology, pausing in Jerusalem, Mecca, Constantinople, Florence, Silicon Valley, and everywhere in between—apart from the Senior Common Rooms of Oxford colleges.
- Make judges and advocates ask: 'How can a judgment about the best interests of a patient be satisfactory unless its basis is made clear?'

Oxford, UK

Charles Foster
Jonathan Herring

Contents

1 What Does the Law Say About Human Thriving? 1
1.1 Introduction 1
1.2 Decisions by Capacitous Adults 2
1.3 Best Interests Determinations on Behalf of Incapacitous Patients 7
1.4 Decision-Making on Behalf of Very Sick Children 16
1.4.1 Thriving Is not Just a Medical Issue 17
1.4.2 Thriving: A Personalised Assessment 18
1.5 The Presumption in Favour of Continued Life 18
1.5.1 The Relationship Between the Parents and Child 20
1.6 Summary in Relation to Decision-Making on Behalf of Children 22
References 22

2 The Idea of Human Thriving: A Brief History 23
2.1 Introduction 23
2.2 Ideas of the Good Life in the Ancient Greek and Roman Worlds 25
2.3 Ideas of the Good Life in the Jewish and Christian Worlds 30
2.4 Ideas of the Good Life in the Renaissance and the Enlightenment 34
2.5 From the Enlightenment to the Present 39
References 42

3 What Makes Humans Happy? 43
3.1 Introduction 43
3.2 Conscious and Unconscious Minds and the Conversation Between Them 44
3.3 The Relevance of Bodily Integrity and Physical Environment 46
3.4 The Significance of Rationality for Human Thriving 47

3.5 Sociality and Thriving 49
3.6 Work and Significance 50
3.7 Whatever Happiness Is, Can It Be Pursued? 51
3.8 Happiness and Virtue 51
3.9 Conclusion 53
References 54

4 Thriving, Care and Vulnerability 57
4.1 Introduction 57
4.2 Vulnerability and Thriving 58
4.3 Mutuality and Vulnerability 59
4.4 Openness and Vulnerability 60
4.5 Relationships and Vulnerability 60
4.6 Personhood and Vulnerability 61
4.7 Autonomy and Vulnerability 62
4.8 Vulnerability and Compassion 64
4.9 Care 64
4.10 Conclusion 66
References 66

5 Making It Work: Ideas of Human Thriving in Practice 69
5.1 Introduction 69
5.2 Scenario 1: Becoming a Wolf 70
5.2.1 The Law 70
5.2.2 Jonathan Herring (JH) 71
5.2.3 Charles Foster (CF) 72
5.3 Scenario 2: Breast Enlargement 73
5.3.1 The Law 73
5.3.2 JH 74
5.3.3 CF 75
5.4 Scenario 3: Permanent Vegetative State 76
5.4.1 The Law 76
5.4.2 JH 77
5.4.3 CF 77
5.5 Scenario 4: Dementia 79
5.5.1 The Law 79
5.5.2 JH 79
5.5.3 CF 80
5.6 Scenario 5: Should Sperm Be Extracted? 81
5.6.1 The Law 81
5.6.2 JH 81
5.6.3 CF 82

5.7 Scenario 6: A Dispute About Education 82
5.7.1 The Law 82
5.7.2 JH 83
5.7.3 CF 84
5.8 Scenario 7: Assisting Suicide 84
5.8.1 The Law 84
5.8.2 JH 85
5.8.3 CF 85
Reference 86

6 Conclusion 87

Chapter 1
What Does the Law Say About Human Thriving?

Abstract This chapter surveys decisions of the English courts in relation to best interests determinations for incapacitous adults and children. The courts never state explicitly what account of human thriving is being assumed. This is problematic. Autonomy, or the potential for future autonomy, is plainly a very important criterion. So is the capacity to experience some pleasures and not to be subject to some vicissitudes. The relationship between acting virtuously, or at least being virtuous, is rarely acknowledged. The model of the self assumed by the law is essentially an atomistic one.

Keywords Capacity · Incapacity · Best interests · Adult · Children

1.1 Introduction

This chapter argues that the English law is a system designed to maximise human thriving. If and insofar as that is not its aim, the law is an intolerable interference with freedom.

We contend that many jurisprudential difficulties are solved if the objective of the law is formulated in this (unusual) way.

Law, we suggest, is about the regulation of decisions. We begin by examining decisions made by capacitous persons. We use this examination to ground our contention about the law as an agent of human thriving, and we look briefly (mainly using the European Convention on Human Rights) at some of the law's substantive averments about what it means to lead a thriving human life.

We then move on to look in more detail at decision-making on behalf of incapacitous patients. Such decisions, in England and Wales, are made in the *best interests* of the patient. One would expect such decisions to be explicit about the account of human thriving that is assumed. Rarely is this so, but sometimes the implicit account can be deduced.

C. Foster and J. Herring, *Human Thriving and the Law*, SpringerBriefs in Law,
https://doi.org/10.1007/978-3-030-01135-2_1

1.2 Decisions by Capacitous Adults

Most adults, of course, are capable of making decisions (if not good decisions) for themselves. Where an adult decides to do something that is not prohibited by the law, the law will not interfere.

In *Schloendorff v Society of New York Hospital* (1914) 105 NE 92 Cardozo J said:

> Every human being of adult years and sound mind has a right to determine what shall be done with his own body.[1]

This principle has been consistently recognised in the English law.[2] Thus, for instance, In *In re T (Adult: Refusal of Treatment,* Butler-Sloss LJ cited with approval this section of the judgment of Robins JA in *Malette v Shulman*[3]*)*:

> The right to determine what shall be done with one's own body is a fundamental right in our society. The concepts inherent in this right are the bedrock upon which the principles of self-determination and individual autonomy are based. Free individual choice in matters affecting this right should, in my opinion, be accorded very high priority.

The priority, indeed, is *near* absolute. Thus in *Re MB (Medical Treatment)* Butler-Sloss LJ said:

> A mentally competent patient has an absolute right to refuse to consent to medical treatment for any reason, rational or irrational, or for no reason at all, even where that decision may lead to his or her own death.[4]

This was a summary of part of Lord Templemans's speech in *Sidaway v Board of Governors of the Bethlem Royal Hospital and the Maudsley Hospital* where he said:

> … the doctor is not entitled to make the final decision with regard to treatment which may have disadvantages or dangers. Where the patient's health and future are at stake, the patient must make the final decision. The patient is free to decide whether or not to submit to treatment recommended by the doctor and therefore the doctor impliedly contracts to provide information which is adequate to enable the patient to reach a balanced judgment, subject always to the doctor's own obligation to say and do nothing which the doctor is satisfied will be harmful to the patient … If the doctor making a balanced judgment advises the patient to submit to the operation, the patient is entitled to reject that advice for reasons which are rational, or irrational, or for no reason. The duty of the doctor in these circumstances, subject to his overriding duty to have regard to the best interests of the patient, is to provide the patient with information which will enable the patient to make a balanced judgment if the patient chooses to make a balanced judgment.[5]

---

[1]At 93.

[2]It was comprehensively reviewed by Munby J in *R (Burke) v General Medical Council* [2004] EWHC 1879 (Admin) cp the Court of Appeal decision in the same case: [2005] EWCA Civ 1003.

[3](1990) 67 DLR (4th) 321, 336.

[4][1997] 2 FLR 426, at 432.

[5][1985] AC 871, at 904.

If this were a complete summary of the law, we would conclude that the law simply equated human thriving with autonomy (whether autonomy is exercised in an objectively responsible way or not), and that there was no more to say about the subject. But things are not so simple.

In *R v Brown*[6] a group of homosexual sado-masochists consensually inflicted injury on one another. They were charged with and convicted of (variously) assault occasioning actual bodily harm[7] and unlawful wounding.[8] They contended that since consent was a defence to these charges, they had been wrongly convicted. Not so, held a majority of the House of Lords[9]: there are some things to which one cannot validly consent.

Lord Templeman (with whom Lords Jauncey and Lowry agreed) concluded that:

> the authorities dealing with the intentional infliction of bodily harm do not establish that consent is a defence to a charge under the 1861 Act. They establish that the courts have accepted that consent is a defence to the infliction of bodily harm in the course of some lawful activities. The question is whether the defence should be extended to the infliction of bodily harm in the course of sadomasochistic encounters.

This, he said could '*only be decided by consideration of policy and public interest.*'

He continued:

> Counsel for the appellants argued that consent should provide a defence to charges under both ss 20 and 47 because, it was said, every person has a right to deal with his body as he pleases. I do not consider that this slogan provides a sufficient guide to the policy decision which must now be made. It is an offence for a person to abuse his own body and mind by taking drugs. Although the law is often broken, the criminal law restrains a practice which is regarded as dangerous and injurious to individuals and which if allowed and extended is harmful to society generally. In any event the appellants in this case did not mutilate their own bodies. They inflicted bodily harm on willing victims. Suicide is no longer an offence but a person who assists another to commit suicide is guilty of murder or manslaughter.
>
> The assertion was made on behalf of the appellants that the sexual appetites of sadists and masochists can only be satisfied by the infliction of bodily harm and that the law should not punish the consensual achievement of sexual satisfaction. There was no evidence to support the assertion that sado-masochist activities are essential to the happiness of the appellants or any other participants but the argument would be acceptable if sado-masochism were only concerned with sex as the appellants contend. In my opinion sado-masochism is not only concerned with sex. Sado-masochism is also concerned with violence. The evidence discloses that the practices of the appellants were unpredictably dangerous and degrading to body and mind and were developed with increasing barbarity and taught to persons whose consents were dubious or worthless.

---

[6][1994] 1 AC 212; see too *Laskey, Jaggard and Brown v United Kingdom* (1997) 24 EHRR 39.

[7]Offences Against the Person Act 1861s. 47.

[8]Offences Against the Person Act 1861s. 20.

[9]Lords Mustill and Slynn dissenting.

Brown has been recently endorsed by the Court of Appeal in *R v BM*—a prosecution for (consensual) tongue-splitting, nipple-excision, and ear removal.[10]

Our bodies, then, are not absolutely our own. We cannot choose to subject them to sadomasochistic torture, to fill them with illegal drugs, or, indeed, to use them to commit any criminal acts. Nor can we fail to use them to discharge any duty that is imposed on us by the law of tort. (Duties under contract are of course rather different, since we can choose not to enter into a contract).

There are, broadly, two reasons for these constraints. Sometimes the two reasons co-exist in the justification for a particular constraint: sometimes only one of them pertains. The reasons are:

(a) *The prohibited acts or omissions are contrary to some notion of what it means to lead a thriving human life.*

In *Brown* this was what was described by Lord Templeman as a 'policy' decision. It might better be described as a philosophical decision. It is, in fact, a decision based on some anthropological assumptions—assumptions about the kind of beings humans are, and hence about the conditions in which they can be properly human. The criminal law and the law of tort are not particularly ambitious: they do not strain to maximise human thriving (that is more properly a political concern). But they do seek to minimise dehumanization to the extent that such damage limitation is consistent with proper respect for autonomy. It may be (and one of us—CF-has contended that it is) that such considerations boil down to a respect for human dignity. Dignity and autonomy are usually allies: respecting dignity usually means honouring autonomy. But there may be occasions when the exercise of autonomy is contrary to human dignity. Where that is so (as the House of Lords found that it was in *Brown*) dignity (being the parent principle from which autonomy—as well as other commonly cited principles such as beneficence and non-maleficence are derived), will trump autonomy.

(b) *Prohibition of the acts or omissions is necessary for the public good*

Where this is the case, the relevant act or omission will usually be one that is condemned on dignity/thriving grounds regardless of whether or not there is some wider societal fall out. It will usually be contrary to the actor's/defaulter's dignity to act or fail to act.

The relevant compromise to the 'public good' will not always be tangible—such as the risk of disease transmission that was mooted in *Brown*. The relevant good may simply be the good of not having intangibly dehumanizing behaviour in society. To find out what that rather amorphous phrase means we need to have a clearly articulated legal anthropology—ideally supported by empirical evidence

---

[10][2018] EWCA Crim 560. For discussion see http://blog.practicalethics.ox.ac.uk/2018/04/tongue-splitting-nipple-excision-and-ear-removal-why-prosecute-the-operator-but-not-the-customer/#more-13304.

about what constitutes human thriving. The empirical support is the subject of Chap. 3.

These arguments are well accommodated within the jurisprudence of Article 8 of the ECHR. Article 8 reads:

> 1. Everyone has the right to respect for his private and family life, his home and his correspondence.
> 2. There shall be no interference by a public authority with the exercise of this right except such as is in accordance with the law and is necessary in a democratic society in the interests of national security, public safety or the economic well-being of the country, for the prevention of disorder or crime, for the protection of health or morals, or for the protection of the rights and freedoms of others.

This is the most elastic of the Convention articles. It is the article within which the notion of autonomy has most fully evolved. Its structure indicates explicitly that individual autonomy is not the whole story: the individual interests protected by 8 (1) must be balanced by the societal interests described in 8(2). Yet it is not accurate to say that there is a stand-off between 8(1) and 8(2). Rather the picture of humans painted by Article 8 as a whole is a picture of humans as necessarily, quintessentially relational, societal creatures who can only thrive individually insofar as they are embedded in a social matrix. Article 8(2) does not contradict 8(1): 8(2) considerations do not trump 8(1) interests. 8(2) considerations rather provide the necessary context in which individual 8(1) considerations can take root and have meaning. Take away the relational context and individual autonomy ceases to be a real good. 'It is not good for the man to be alone', opines God in the Hebrew Bible.[11] The ECtHR tends to agree.

Another way of putting this is to say that the law sees the individual endorsement and honouring of a social contract as a necessary prerequisite of individual thriving, or that the law's model of a human being is an essentially communitarian one—in which it is impossible to describe a person (and so describe her rights and duties) except in terms of the nexus of relationships in which she exists. We argue for this communitarian model of legal personality elsewhere: (Foster and Herring 2017). We see Article 8 as a legal exposition of Mill's famous dictum: '*The only purpose for which power can be rightfully exercised over any member of a civilized community, against his will, is to prevent harm to others. His own good, either physical or moral, is not a sufficient warrant. He cannot rightfully be compelled to do or to forbear because it will be better for him to do so, because it will make him happier, because, in the opinions of others, to do so would be wise, or even right.*[12]'

The law seeks to promote human thriving. It does so in many ways. The criminal law truncates autonomy in order to maximise human thriving. It inhibits (for instance) the freedom of X to punch Y in the face, or to enter Y's property and take her goods, because it has decided that the net amount of human thriving will be increased if Y's face remains unpunched and her house unburgled. In prohibiting

[11]Genesis 2:18.

[12]*On Liberty.*

murder the law is asserting both that being alive is, with some caveats, good, and that a murderer is acting in a way inconsistent with the human thriving of his victim, and with the thriving of society at large, and with his own thriving. To act as a murderer acts is not good for a murderer—even if he avoids detection and punishment. If human thriving can be cast in terms of human dignity (and our discussion of *Brown* suggests that it can), Mountfield and Singh's comment is apposite: Dignity, they say, is 'Janus-faced'.[13] If X diminishes the dignity/thriving of Y, X's dignity/thriving is diminished too—and probably more than Y's.

The law of contract assumes that, usually, human thriving will be maximised if contractual promises are kept—even though that interferes with the freedom to break a promise. The law of tort imposes duties—and hence restricts freedoms—because it has calculated that this increases human thriving.

As we have already observed in the context of Article 8 of the ECHR, an analysis in terms of rights rather than duties comes to the same conclusion. It is worth making the trite observation that the Convention is entitled the European Convention on *Human* Rights, and is grafted into the English law by the *Human* Rights Act 1998. For this implies that there is something about being human which generates rights: it is saying that something about the type of being that humans are means that they thrive best if they are credited with certain rights. It's essentially an anthropological assertion, with corollaries in moral philosophy. Thus humans thrive if they are alive,[14] if they are not tortured or subjected to inhuman (there's that anthropology again, with its normative baggage) or degrading treatment or punishment,[15] if they are not enslaved or made to perform forced labour,[16] if their liberty and security are protected,[17] if they are tried fairly,[18] if they are not punished except in accordance with the law,[19] if their private and family lives are respected,[20] if they have freedom of thought, conscience, and religion,[21] if they have freedom of expression,[22] if they can freely assemble and associate,[23] if they are allowed to marry and to found a family,[24] and if they are not discriminated against.[25] It goes without saying that these rights apply to incapacitous as well as capacitous patients.

---

[13]*Cited Baroness Hale, 'Dignity',* Journal of Social Welfare and Family Law *(2009): 31; 101.*

[14]ECHR Article 2.

[15]ECHR Article 3.

[16]ECHR Article 4.

[17]ECHR Article 5.

[18]ECHR Article 6.

[19]ECHR Article 7.

[20]ECHR Article 8.

[21]ECHR Article 9.

[22]ECHR Article 10.

[23]ECHR Article 11.

[24]ECHR Article 12.

[25]ECHR Article 14.

1.3 Best Interests Determinations on Behalf of Incapacitous Patients

Some people cannot make decisions for themselves because of some legal incapacity (for instance if they are a child)[26] or mental incapacity.

An adult is regarded as unable to make a decision for herself if she is unable:

(a) to understand the information relevant to the decision,
(b) to retain that information,
(c) to use or weigh that information as part of the process of making the decision, or
(d) to communicate [her] decision (whether by talking, using sign language or any other means).[27]

The Mental Capacity Act 1985 provides that 'an act done, or decision made, under this Act for or on behalf of a person who lacks capacity must be done, or made, in [her] best interests'.[28]

Every day many thousands of determinations are made about the 'best interests' of incapacitous people. The overwhelming majority of these are made by carers or clinicians (for instance about what the patient should have for her supper, or whether she should be given antibiotics for an infection). A tiny minority (but still a substantial number) are made by judges. Whether the determination is made by a layperson or by the court, it necessarily entails the decision-maker coming to a normative conclusion about what it means to thrive as a human. To make a best interests determination is to say: 'This act will maximise the thriving of the patient.'

One might therefore expect the law to have formulated a clear legal anthropology (specifying what type of creature a human is) and to have identified what it means for a human to thrive. Both might be done by reference to the very considerable body of empirical work referred to in Chap. 3. Yet neither is the case. This is unsatisfactory on many levels. It means (for instance) that the values of individual judicial (or other) decision-makers can intrude inappropriately into best interests determinations. Failure to refer explicitly to the best interests criteria being used means that the basis of judgments is unclear, making evaluation and appeal very difficult.

Sometimes, however, despite the absence of any clear statement of the basis of a decision, it is possible to read, between the lines of judgments, some of the normative assumptions being used.

What follows is an attempt to read between those lines, using best interests determinations about medical treatment decisions in relation to incapacitous adults and children.

---

[26]The law in relation to children's capacity to make decisions is beyond the scope of this book, but see Gillick and Act.

[27]Mental Capacity Act 2005s. 3(1).

[28]s. 1(5).

Best interests: a holistic determination

The Mental Capacity Act 2005 refers simply to the 'best interests' of the patient, and requires this to be ascertained by taking a number of bearings.[29]

The Act requires a holistic determination of best interests. Lady Hale put it this way: '*The most that can be said, therefore, is that in considering the best interests of this particular patient at this particular time, decision-makers must look at his welfare in the widest sense, not just medical but social and psychological....*[30]'

In *Re A (Male Sterilisation)*,[31] Butler-Sloss LJ stated that 'best interests encompasses medical, emotional and all other welfare issues', and in *Re S (Adult Patient: Sterilisation)*[32] Thorpe LJ said that *'[i]n deciding what is best....the judge must have regard to....welfare as the paramount consideration. That embraces issues far wider than the medical. Indeed it would be undesirable and probably impossible to set bounds to what is relevant to a welfare determination.*'

Best interests determinations are (theoretically) objective

There is one (notionally) correct answer to the question: 'Is this intervention in X's best interests?'

This is clear from the relevant legislation. Thus the Mental Capacity Act 2005 provides that: 'An act done, or decision made, under this Act for or on behalf of a person who lacks capacity must be done, or made, in his best interests.'[33] There is no room in this formulation for several equally acceptable answers to the question.

Section 4(1) makes an identical assumption. It begins: 'In determining for the purposes of this Act what is in a person's best interests...'

So far as statutory construction is concerned the position in relation to children is less obvious: Section 1(1) of the Children Act 1989 provides that: 'When a court determines any question with respect to (a)the upbringing of a child; or (b)the administration of a child's property or the application of any income arising from it, the child's welfare shall be the court's paramount consideration.' But it is clear from judicial consideration of this section that, as under the Mental Capacity Act, there is, again, one theoretically correct solution in child welfare cases.

To say as a matter of jurisprudential principle that there is one right answer in each case is one thing. To arrive at it is quite another. Lord Mustill, in *Airedale NHS Trust v Bland,* thought that it was impossible for judges to exclude their own views:

> ....when the intellectual part of the task is complete and the decision-maker has to choose the factors which he will take into account, attach relevant weights to them and then strike a balance the judge is no better equipped, though no worse, than anyone else. In the end it is a

[29]See s. 4: for discussion, see below.

[30]*Aintree University Hospitals v James* * at [39].

[31][2000] 1 FLR 549.

[32][2001] Fam 15.

[33]s. 1(5).

> matter of personal choice, dictated by his or her background, upbringing, education, convictions and temperament.[34]

No doubt complete judicial objectivity, though desirable, is impossible. But some of Lord Mustill's concerns can and should be addressed. In particular it is possible to specify the factors that the decision-maker should take into account, and to be systematic about the way in which they are balanced. Indeed, since *Bland,* the Mental Capacity Act 2005 has sought to specify at least some of the relevant factors[35] and to propose a system for ascertaining best interests,[36] and the 'balance sheet' approach (in which the benefits and detriments associated with a proposed course of action or inaction are listed and weighted, giving a positive or negative score) has been repeatedly endorsed by the courts.[37] We examine some of the Mental Capacity Act's best interests criteria below, and note that those criteria have been expounded and expanded by the courts.

The presumption in favour of the maintenance of life

There is a strong, though rebuttable, presumption that life is a good thing and should be maintained. Often this has been articulated in terms of the doctrine of the sanctity of life. Thus, for instance, Hoffmann LJ in *Airedale NHS Trust v Bland* said this:

> I start with the concept of the sanctity of life … [W]e have a strong feeling that there is an intrinsic value in human life, irrespective of whether it is valuable to the person concerned or indeed to anyone else. Those who adhere to religious faiths which believe in the sanctity of all God's creation and in particular that human life was created in the image of God himself will have no difficulty with the concept of the intrinsic value of human life. But even those without any religious belief think in the same way. In a case like this we should not try to analyse the rationality of such feelings. What matters is that, in one form or another, they form part of almost everyone's intuitive values. No law which ignores them can possibly hope to be acceptable.
>
> Our belief in the sanctity of life explains why we think it is almost always wrong to cause the death of another human being, even one who is terminally ill or so disabled that we think that if we were in his position we would rather be dead. Still less do we tolerate laws

---

[34]At 887.

[35]See the discussion below.

[36]See s. 4.

[37]See, e.g., Thorpe LJ in *Re A (Male Sterilisation)* supra, at 560: '*There can be no doubt in my mind that the evaluation of best interests is akin to a welfare appraisal…Pending the enactment of a checklist or other statutory direction it seems to me that the first instance judge with the responsibility to make an evaluation of the best interests of a claimant lacking capacity should draw up a balance sheet. The first entry should be of any factor or factors of actual benefit.....Then on the other sheet the judge should write any counterbalancing dis-benefits to the applicant…Then the judge should enter on each sheet the potential gains and losses in each instance making some estimate of the extent of the possibility that the gain or loss might accrue. At the end of that exercise the judge should be better placed to strike a balance between the sum of the certain and possible gains against the sum of the certain and possible losses. Obviously, only if the account is in relatively significant credit will the judge conclude that the application is likely to advance the best interests of the claimant.*'

> such as existed in Nazi Germany, by which handicapped people or inferior races could be put to death because someone else thought that their lives were useless.[38]

This principle has been repeatedly endorsed by the courts,[39] and is an expression of the state's obligations under Article 2 of the ECHR.

But it is not absolute. After the passage in *Bland* cited above, Hoffmann LJ continued:

> But the sanctity of life is only one of a cluster of ethical principles which we apply to decisions about how we should live. Another is respect for the individual human being and in particular for his right to choose how he should live his own life. We call this individual autonomy or the right of self-determination. And another principle, closely connected, is respect for the dignity of the individual human being: our belief that quite irrespective of what the person concerned may think about it, it is wrong for someone to be humiliated or treated without respect for his value as a person. The fact that the dignity of an individual is an intrinsic value is shown by the fact that we feel embarrassed and think it wrong when someone behaves in a way which we think demeaning to himself, which does not show sufficient respect for himself as a person.[40]

In the law in general, as in this citation, autonomy is at the front of the queue of principles that can rebut the presumption that life should be maintained.

Autonomy/self-determination

Autonomy is the main principle at work in the Mental Capacity Act 2005. Thus, for instance, a decision-maker must, 'so far as reasonably practicable, permit and encourage the person to participate, or to improve his ability to participate, as fully as possible in any act done for him and any decision affecting him'[41] and must consider, so far as is reasonably ascertainable—

> (a) the person's past and present wishes and feelings (and, in particular, any relevant written statement made by him when he had capacity), (b) the beliefs and values that would be likely to influence his decision if he had capacity, and
>
> (c) the other factors that he would be likely to consider if he were able to do so.[42]

Wishes expressed in advance directives are regarded as definitive of best interests if the advance directive is 'valid and applicable' and if (in the case of an advance directive relating to the withdrawal or withholding of life-sustaining treatment) certain formalities are complied with.[43]

---

[38][1993] AC 789 at 826.

[39]See, for instance, *Aintree University Hospitals v James* [2013] UKSC 67, per Lady Hale at [35]. For an example of the principle's application, see *St. George's Healthcare NHS Trust v P* [2015] COPLR 561.

[40]ibid.

[41]s. 4(4).

[42]s. 4(6).

[43]See sections 24, 25 and 26. But note the tension between s 4(6)(a) (which requires past and present wishes to be 'consider[ed]', and s. 26, which purports to make past wishes, in the form of an advance directive, binding in some circumstances.

Although the best interests test applies, it is clear (as the Supreme Court has confirmed)[44] that there is a strong element of substituted judgment—whereby the decision-maker considers what the patient would do were they able to make a decision for themselves.[45]

Reliance on autonomy implies an assertion about identity

The law tends to assume that there is no difficulty about identifying the patient: that the patient whose name is on the birth certificate is, for all legal purposes, the patient in the hospital bed, and the patient whose name will be on the death certificate. We have interrogated that assumption at length (Foster and Herring 2017), and do not repeat the argument here. We merely note that our preferences vary widely depending on, inter alia, the role that we assume or the circumstances in which we find ourselves. Disease or injury may change radically our priorities and preferences. A patient with Alzheimer's disease may have very little psychological continuity with her pre-disease self. We have contended (with some important caveats) that the object of legal consideration should be the patient as she is at the time that a decision comes to be made on her behalf, rather than the notional patient whose views may be expressed in (for instance) an advance directive and who for all practical purposes has been superseded by the post-injury or post-disease patient. This has led us to urge caution in the construction of advance directives: they can be documents which tyrannise (sometimes fatally) a patient who has only a tenuous connection with the maker of the advance directive. We consider that this view draws support from the insistence of the Mental Capacity Act that the decision-maker considers the 'best interests' of the patient: note the present tense. The relevant patient is the one in the clinic: the relevant interests are primarily those of the patient in the clinic—though, as we have noted, previously expressed wishes are relevant to the assessment of those interests.

Nonetheless, the courts have repeatedly recognised that an interest pertinent to the overall best interests assessment is the interest in being remembered a particular way. Sir Thomas Bingham MR noted in *Bland* that '*An objective assessment of Mr. Bland's best interests, viewed through his eyes,*[46] *would in my opinion give weight to....the desire he would naturally have to be remembered as a cheerful, carefree, gregarious teenager and not an object of pity....*[47]'

---

[44]See *Aintree University Hospitals v James,* ibid, per Lady Hale at [24].

[45]A good example of the exercise of subsituted judgement is in the judgment of Charles J in *Re Briggs* [2017] 4 WLR 37 at [111]: *'Members of the family told me that in their view Mr. Briggs would regard his present situation as horrible and one that he would not wish to continue. Included within the reasons given are that a life in which he did not have the ability to communicate with his wife and child is not one that he would be wishing to have...'* This evidence weighed heavily with the judge in making his best interests determination.

[46]'...through his eyes': another endorsement of substituted judgment.

[47]Ibid, 813.

Lord Hoffman in *Bland* put the same point slightly differently:

> I think that the fallacy in [the Official Solicitor's] argument is that it assumes that we have no interests except in those things of which we have conscious experience. But this does not accord with most people's intuitive feelings about their lives and deaths. At least part of the reason why we honour the wishes of the dead about the distribution of their property is that we think it would wrong them not to do so, despite the fact that we believe that they will never know that their will has been ignored. Most people would like an honourable and dignified death and we think it wrong to dishonour their deaths, even when they are unconscious that it is happening. We pay respect to their dead bodies and to their memory because we think it an offence against the dead themselves if we do not…[48]

Note the assumption in both these passages: the Tony Bland in the hospital bed, and indeed in the mortuary, is crucially and quintessentially identical with the Tony Bland in his pre-injury condition, and accordingly to act in the best interests of the post-injury patient is to act in a way that would be endorsed by the pre-injury patient.

Lord Mustill, again in *Bland,* was even more emphatic: '…the continued treatment of Anthony Bland can no longer serve to maintain that combination of manifold characteristics that we call a personality….'[49] And, therefore, continued treatment was not in Bland's best interests. By 'a personality' Lord Mustill plainly meant 'Tony Bland's pre-accident personality.'

In *Re Briggs,*[50] a case involving a patient in Minimally Conscious State as a result of brain and other injuries, Charles J was heavily influenced by the fact that the patient's wife and other family members said that 'as a result of his brain damage Mr. Briggs is now a different person who will not have insight into his previous wishes, feelings, beliefs, values, approach to life, and the impact on him of the brain injury…'[51] The object of legal interest, therefore (the pre-accident Mr. Briggs) had effectively ceased to exist, and *that* entity accordingly had no persisting interest in survival.

Relationality

As a matter of biological and sociological fact we are relational beings. We played no part in our conception or gestation, little in our upbringings, and at the end of life are likely to be dependent on others for our basic needs. And at all times between birth and death, despite our vaunted autonomy, we are in fact dependent—on doctors, lawmakers, pilots, other road-users, cooks, and so on. We are likely to get our ethics and our law less wrong if we acknowledge these facts.

The law has traditionally been reluctant to acknowledge that humans are not discrete, atomistic entities. That is the way that they have been perceived in the law of contract (where there is no difficulty in identifying the individual parties to

[48]ibid at 829.

[49]ibid at 899.

[50][2017] 4 WLR 37.

[51][99]. See too *Re N* [2016] COPLR 88; and *Sheffield Teaching Hospitals NHS Foundation Trust v TH* [2014] EWCOP 4.

transactions), the law of tort (where X owes a duty to Y, and the identity of X and Y is always clear), in crime (where, with a few exceptions such as insanity and automatism, individual responsibility is assumed), and in the doctor-patient relationship (traditionally construed in a quasi-contractual way, with all the associated assumptions about the non-porous nature of the boundary that surrounds each of the parties).

But there are signs that these assumptions are dissolving and giving way to a view of the person that is far more communitarian, and far more concordant with the real facts of embodied human life.

In *Re G (Children),*[52] Munby LJ noted that:

> Herring and Foster have argued persuasively ('Welfare means rationality, virtue and altruism', (2012) 32 Legal Studies 480), that behind a judicial determinations of welfare there lies an essentially Aristotelian notion of the 'good life'.....
>
> The well-being of a child cannot be assessed in isolation. Human beings live within a network of relationships. Men and women are sociable beings. (…) As Herring and Foster comment, relationships are central to our sense and understanding of ourselves. Our characters and understandings of ourselves from the earliest days are charted by reference to our relationships with others. It is only by considering the child's network of relationships that their well-being can be properly considered. So a child's relationships, both within and without the family, are always relevant to the child's interests; often they will be determinative.

The capacity for relationship often features prominently in best interests determinations. In *James,* Lady Hale noted that '…great weight had to be given to Mr. James' family life which was 'of the closest and most meaningful kind.''[53] And in *Re M (Incapacitated Person: Withdrawal of Treatment)*[54] (which concerned a patient in a Minimally Conscious State as a result of Huntingdon's disease), Peter Jackson J was heavily influenced in his decision about whether continued clinically assisted nutrition and hydration was in the patient's best interests by the evidence of the patient's mother who said that '*M is rarely awake and all I can describe is a 'body on a bed'…Even when she is awake M makes no sign of recognition and does not look at me or engage with me….for around 18 months now I have seen nothing which makes me think that she has any awareness of what is going on whatsoever….*'

A few other citations will make the point. Amongst the evidence identified by judges as relevant to best interests is:

- No speech. Apparent ability to be able, sometimes, to follow simple sentences. Squeezing of son's hand when it was placed in hers. May nod when wishes to affirm. Often no response to questions. Does not appear to listen to the radio or

[52] [2012] EWCA Civ 1233.

[53] ibid, at [40].

[54] [2018] 1 WLR 465.

watch TV. Occasionally smiles. (*PL v (1) Sutton Clinical Commissioning Group (2) Royal Borough of Kingston Upon Thames*).[55]

- Possible awareness from time to time of the presence of children at the bedside, holding the patient's hands. (*Abertawe Bro Morgannwg University LHB v RY*).[56]
- Family believed that the patient responded to words from family members, to the smell of perfume, and to physical touch. Sensitive to touch on the hands and face.[57] (*An NHS Trust v L, FL and TL*).
- The patient could fix and track objects within her line of vision, but had little or no recognition of what the object might be. She had no other awareness. (*Re N*)[58]
- The patient made sounds interpreted by her carers as indicating when she wanted something done. The carers thought that the patient was sometimes aware of different people being present, that she smiled in response to some speech, and that she responded to people talking about her. She appeared to look at objects and track them. Very occasionally responded verbally to speech, for instance: 'Are you going to say good morning to X? Reply: 'Morning.' The patient stuck her tongue out to ask for her teeth to be cleaned. She occasionally spoke words such as 'hello', 'where am I?', and 'bloody hell'. (*Re W*)[59]
- Inconsistent and often delayed ability to follow motor instructions—necessitating a good deal of rousing, verbal instruction, and encouragement. Could localise a voice. Possible communication by way of facial expression in relation to familiar conversations and topics. (*St. George's Healthcare NHS Trust v P*).[60]

We have argued elsewhere (Foster and Herring 2016) that an essential part of thriving as a human in society—an essential part of the Good Life—is to act altruistically. It is of the nature of humans that they act self-sacrificingly. A benefit altruistically surrendered may become more of a benefit than before—or at least be prevented from being transformed into a detriment.

It has long been recognised that apparently altruistic behaviour might be in the best interests of a patient, but in the past such apparent altruism has been construed in the law—just as incidents of apparent altruism in biology have been construed—as disguised self-interest. Thus, for instance, donation of bone marrow by X to save her sibling, Y, has been read as being in X's best interests because, absent the transplant, X would be deprived of the benefit of Y's company, or might later suffer the detriment of feeling guilty at not having been the means of saving Y when she might have done.

---

[55][2017] EWCOP 22.

[56][2017] COPLR 143.

[57][2013] COPLR 558.

[58][2016] COPLR 88.

[59][2011] EWHC 2443 (Fam).

[60][2015] COPLR 561.

There are signs, however, that genuine altruism—altruism for altruism's sake, irrespective of any tangible benefit to the altruist—might be acknowledged by the courts as a benefit.

Thus in *James* Lady Hale acknowledged that in considering, within the ambit of the best interests assessment, what the patient might have wanted for themselves, it might be legitimate to include assessing the patient's individual best interests it might include 'altruistic sentiments and concern for others.'[61] In *Re Briggs*[62] Charles J noted that amongst the factors that indicated what the patient would have wanted were 'the interests of other people who [the patient] would have been likely to take into account and so, for example, many if not most [patients] when they had capacity would have taken into account their relationships with others (e.g. spouse and children), how they think their children should be parented and the impact on those closest to them of what they decide to do.'

There is one important caveat. One expression of altruism relates to resource allocation. To maintain a severely injured patient consumes resources that could save or materially enhance the life of others. A more robust application of the principles of relationality and altruism might suggest that it is the best interests of X for X's life-sustaining treatment to be discontinued in order for the resources to be released for the use of others. While the courts have endorsed policy-level decisions about resource allocation they have refused to take resource-allocation issues into account in making decisions about the fate of individual patients.[63] This is intellectually uncomfortable, although we suggest that it is the right ethical approach.

Benefits and detriments: pains and pleasures

We have noted already that the 'balance sheet' approach is routinely used in making best interests determinations. This approach assumes that it is possible to identify what is a benefit and what is a detriment. The identification may be affected by the patient's own actual or assumed views: a blood transfusion of obvious medical benefit might be a detriment to a Jehovah's Witness who may think that the temporal benefit is massively outweighed by the eternal detriment.

The identification of benefits and detriments plainly makes a number of normative assumptions about what it is good and not good for humans to experience. We look in Chap. 3 at the extent to which those assumptions are supported by the empirical evidence about human happiness. But for the moment we merely observe that the judges (entirely unsurprisingly) agree about what constitute benefits and detriments. Relationality is a benefit, and accordingly the absence of the ability to enter into relationship is a detriment (as we have already seen). The ability to make choices is a benefit (in *Re Briggs*, the ability to choose what colour tee-shirt to wear

---

[61]ibid, at [24], following para 3.31 of the Law Commission in their *Report on Mental Incapacity* (1995, Law Com No 231). The 2005 Act is substantially based on this Report.

[62]Supra, at [56].

[63]See *Bland,* supra.

was cited as an example).[64] Pain, depression and physical handicap are detriments. Various intellectual and sensory pleasures have been identified as benefits: the ability to enjoy watching tennis on TV, the ability to respond to the sun and wind on the face, and the sight of a lake, and crying in response to music.[65]

Summary in relation to incapacitous adults

We have surveyed some of the main cases which indicate how the judges view the Good Life. We have suggested that concordance with the Good Life is sometimes expressed in terms of human dignity, and informs all judicial best interests determinations. Respect for autonomy (in terms of respect for previously expressed wishes and in terms of substituted judgment) is crucially important, but is not the whole story. It is important to ask *who* the patient is: this may be modified by medical or other circumstances. Relationality is central to human thriving, and altruism may be an important expression of relationality. There is general judicial agreement about what amount to benefits and detriments.

1.4 Decision-Making on Behalf of Very Sick Children

This section explores the concept of thriving as applied by the courts when considering the cases of very sick children. This might seem a strange area of the law to examine. However, it is helpful because it strips humanity back to its core. To be blunt: in many of these cases the courts are considering when life is worse than death. Or what form of human life is better than no life at all. These cases, therefore, indicate what the law regards as the most basic forms of flourishing.

There is now extensive case law on these issues. The kind of case that will be considered here is where a child is extremely sick and is being kept alive through medical intervention. The question that typically arises is whether to withdraw that intervention—which would inevitably result in the death of the child. Where the parents agree, it is unlikely the law will become involved. It is usually where the parents disagree that the courts will be required to resolve the dispute. These cases are typically brought as applications for a declaration by the court that the doctor's proposed course of action is lawful. The legal test to be applied is straightforward: will the order promote the child's best interests? The courts have been clear that it is for them, rather than the parents, to determine a child's best interests. This was well captured by Holman J in *An NHS Trust v A*[66] when he said that parents' wishes 'are wholly irrelevant to consideration of the objective best interests of the child save to the extent in any given case that they may illuminate the quality and value to the child of the child/parent relationship.'

64ibid, at [51].

65*Re W,* ibid.

66[2007] EWHC 1744.

The emphasis on best interests has recently been confirmed by the Supreme Court in *Evans v Alder Hay Hospital*[67]:

> The gold standard, by which most of these decisions are reached, is an assessment of his best interests. The first provision in the Children Act is that the child's welfare shall be the court's paramount consideration. Parliament's provision reflects international instruments, particularly the UN Convention on the Rights of the Child. And in the Human Rights Convention, the rights of a child under article 8 will, if inconsistent with the rights of his parents, prevail over them.

Despite being the 'gold standard' it must be admitted that the concept of best interests is notoriously nebulous. The courts have been clear that 'best interests' are not limited to medical best interests. The courts' analysis of best interests has much to tell us about the judicial understanding of thriving. Several points emerge.

1.4.1 Thriving Is not Just a Medical Issue

The Court of Appeal in *Wyatt v Portsmouth NHS Trust*[68] set out the key factors to be considered in a best interests assessment:

> The judge must decide what is in the child's best interests. In making that decision, the welfare of the child is paramount, and the judge must look at the question from the assumed point of view of the patient (Re J). There is a strong presumption in favour of a course of action which will prolong life, but that presumption is not irrebuttable (Re J). The term 'best interests' encompasses medical, emotional, and all other welfare issues (Re A). The court must conduct a balancing exercise in which all the relevant factors are weighed (Re J) and a helpful way of undertaking this exercise is to draw up a balance sheet (Re A).

This broad approach has received support from Lady Hale in *Aintree University Hospitals NHS Foundation Trust v James*, albeit in relation to the assessment of the best interests of adults who lack capacity[69]:

> in considering the best interests of this particular patient at this particular time, decision-makers must look at his welfare in the widest sense, not just medical but social and psychological; they must consider the nature of the medical treatment in question, what it involves and its prospects of success; they must consider what the outcome of that treatment for the patient is likely to be; they must try and put themselves in the place of the individual patient and ask what his attitude to the treatment is or would be likely to be; and they must consult others who are looking after him or interested in his welfare, in particular for their view of what his attitude would be.

This approach is, perhaps, inevitable. These cases often reply on an assessment of whether the pain a child is experiencing is outweighed by the pleasures a child can experience. This is not, in essence, a medical question. The difficulty for the

---

[67] https://www.supremecourt.uk/cases/docs/alfie-evans-reasons-200318.pdf; para 14.

[68] [2005] EWCA Civ 1181, [85].

[69] [2013] UKSC 67, [39].

courts has been that once one departs from the medical facts, assessments become harder—more metaphysical. As Hedley J put it at first instance in *Portsmouth Hospitals NHS Trust v Wyatt*[70]: 'The infinite variety of the human condition never ceases to surprise and it is that fact that defeats any attempt to be more precise in a definition of best interests'.

1.4.2 Thriving: A Personalised Assessment

The courts have made it clear that the best interests assessment is personal to the particular child. Williams J captured this well in the case of *A NHS Trust v Mr and Mrs* S[71] where he stated that:

> a host of matters must all go into the balance when the judge seeks to arrive at his objective assessment of whether **this** treatment is in **this** patient's best interests.... In considering all of these matters, I have very much had in mind what L might want.[72]

This is in line with the general application of the welfare test: the courts have eschewed presumptions about what is generally in the best interests of children, and instead encourage judges to consider the welfare of the particular child in the case (Herring 2016).

1.5 The Presumption in Favour of Continued Life

The recent case law, we suggest, indicates that, at least in child cases, decreasing weight is attached to the idea that simply being alive is a benefit. The courts, though, still talk of a 'presumption' in favour of life. In recent times the presumption has always been held to be rebuttable. In 1991 Lord Donaldson of Lymington in *Re J (A minor) (wardship: medical treatment)*[73] explained:

> We all believe in and assert the sanctity of human life .... Even very severely handicapped people find a quality of life rewarding which to the unhandicapped may seem manifestly intolerable. People have an amazing adaptability. But in the end there will be cases in which the answer must be that it is not in the interests of the child to subject it to treatment which will cause it increased suffering and produce no commensurate benefit, giving the fullest possible weight to the child's, and mankind's desire to survive.

More recently the presumption is simply listed as one factor amongst many and seems to play a minimal role in the reasoning when compared with evidence about

---

[70]*An NHS Foundation Trust v AB, CD and EF* [2005] 1 FLR 21, 23.

[71][2017] EWHC 3619 (Fam), [28], [54].

[72]Original emphasis.

[73][1991] Fam 33.

harms or benefits to the child of treatment or non-treatment. Consider, for example, as a good example of the more modern approach to the presumption the comments of MacDonald J in *Kings College Hospital NHS Foundation Trust v Thomas*[74]:

> a comparison must be drawn between the course advocated by Isaiah's treating doctors, of being allowed to die peacefully with appropriate palliation if, as is inevitable, that is the natural course that Isaiah condition follows, and the course advocated by Isaiah's parents, of a continuation of invasive treatment that will lead only to life being sustained without hope of recovery, with little or no quality of life and with the prospect of infection and increasing physical contortion.

Given it is in the nature of these cases that invasive treatment is required to keep the child alive, we can see there almost being a presumption (in the absence of any other evidence) of withdrawing invasive treatment. Notably even if there is a 'little quality of life' MacDonald J was not convinced the invasive treatment justified it. His application of this principle is interesting:

> The presumption that life should be preserved is not irrebuttable. That it is not recognises that life cannot be, and indeed should not be preserved at all costs in the face of its natural conclusion. Isaiah's life is sustained mechanically and without mechanical ventilation he will die. The burden on Isaiah of that irreversible position is a grave one. If kept alive he will continue to suffer from profound cognitive impairment, extremely severe global motor disability with spastic quadriplegic cerebral palsy. That situation will not change.

While this might appear to be an argument that this suffering is such that it outweighs the presumption of being kept life, what counts as 'suffering' for MacDonald J is, to put it politely, wide. It is not clear that to have a profound cognitive impairment or motor disability amounts to 'suffering'. People with profound cognitive or physical disability impairments can be very happy. The suffering identified does not seem to be the 'pain and suffering' that earlier judgments suggested might rebut the presumption.[75] It may be that McDonald J is suggesting that a life has value insofar as it produces something positive for an individual, and that a severe impairment which prevents the capacity to have any experience means the life does not have value.

That is also a very plausible reading of *Evans v Alder Hey Children's NHS Hospital*,[76] (the Alfie Evans case) where the court explained that 'the scan signals indicated an entirely fluid content to the area that would be occupied by the child's brain, the fluid either being water or cerebral spinal fluid.'[77] Counsel for the parents argued that 'for life to be allowed to carry on and be sustained where it causes no pain to the individual and is of no direct threat to the individual is not contrary to the best interests principle.'[78] This seems to have been an invocation of the presumption in favour of the maintenance of life. If Alfie was incapable of feeling pain

---

[74][2018] EWHC 127 (Fam), [109].

[75]*An NHS Trust v MB & Anor [2006] EWHC 507 (Fam).*

[76][2018] EWCA 984 (Civ).

[77]At [1].

[78]Para 22.

it is not clear what was rebutting the presumption. Yet the court authorized the withdrawal of life-sustaining treatment. This authorisation seems to have been based on the finding that there was no benefit to be gained from continued treatment. This may indicate that the presumption in favour of life is losing its legal significance.

1.5.1 The Relationship Between the Parents and Child

A particularly significant feature of the welfare/best interests assessments in recent cases is the weight attached to the relationship between the parents and child (Bridgeman 2008, 232). The relationship between child and parent is central to the child's identity and is her primary point of reference to the world. This is especially true of younger children. The wellbeing of children is generally bound up with that of their parents. We cannot readily disentangle the welfare of parents and the wellbeing of children (Herring 2014).

A good example of the increasing significance of the parent-child relationship to welfare assessments is *An NHS Trust v MB & Anor*,[79] where Holman J sided with the parents, and did not authorise the withdrawal of life-sustaining treatment. What is of particular interest in this case was that the child appeared to have very limited awareness. He seemed to be suffering relatively little in his greatly impaired state. The treatment was justified so that the boy could 'continue to have a relationship of value to him with his family, and… continue to gain other pleasures from touch, sight and sound.' Holman J noted that the mother had been with the child almost continually.

> He is blessed with parents, especially his mother, but his father, too, who have the time and ability, and also the willingness and commitment to spend long periods of time with him—most of his waking day. So the pleasure which I assume he gains from the relationship is not short lived or occasional, but is available to him as a constant part of his life for long periods of every day.[80]

The relationship generated part of the value of MB's life.

Another indicative case is *NHS Trust v Baby X*[81] where a young boy was profoundly brain damaged and kept alive by ventilation. He was fed by a naso-gastric tube. The staff at the hospital decided that ventilation should be withdrawn. The parents objected. The parents thought that there were signs of improvement, and their religious faith prevented them consenting to a procedure which would lead to the child's death. The court sided with the doctors, but Hedley J placed weight on the need for a good death. He contrasted:

---

[79][2006] EWHC 507 (Fam).

[80][67].

[81][2012] EWHC 2188 (Fam).

death in the arms and presence of parents and a death wired up to machinery and so isolated from all human contact in the course of futile treatment.

It is notable here that the parent-child relationship played a key role in the welfare assessment, in a way not desired by the parents. It may be relevant that Hedley J put greatest weight on the hands-on caring the parents could offer at the time that X died, th, whereas the parents were focused on their hopes for a miracle.

The same point was made in *An NHS Trust v Mr and Mr S*[82] where it was said that:

I have very much had in mind what L might want and I also have tried to take into account what her parents want and I believe that this approach does that. It means that for L and her parents, all avenues to sustain and prolong life, by which I mean a life which is more than simple functioning of organs, but a life which contains interaction and emotional benefit for her will have been tried. It will mean L will have the benefits of her parents and family and their comfort while being largely insulated from pain and distress because palliative care and medication will address that.

Here we see that the potential for social interaction and relational benefits is emphasized: it is a key feature of welfare in these kinds of cases.

As Jo Bridgeman emphasises, solutions to these troublesome cases require careful attention to the individual relationships concerned and the responsibilities that arise from them (Bridgeman 2008, Chap. 1). Solutions should be fashioned from the relationships themselves because, whatever else happens in relation to medical decisions, the child and his or her carers will need to continue in their relationships together: those relationships are worth more than any abstract legal rights. The rights exist to buttress the relationships. In cases involving disputes between doctors and parents this requires the courts to undertake the kinds of sensitive welfare assessment we have seen them taking. In cases involving mature children this involves a careful consideration of both parents' and children's interests in the particular context. There is no automatic bias towards any one party. This is facilitated by Lord Donaldson's approach, which indicates that the doctor, before deciding simply to act on the basis of parental consent, should consider her broader ethical duties and constraints.

The weight attached to the relationship between parent and child in a best interests assessment has caused concern in some cases. In *Re T (A Minor) (Wardship: Medical Treatment)*[83] a child had a life threatening liver complaint. The medical experts advised a liver transplant. Without a transplant, the child would not live much beyond two and a half years: with a transplant the prognosis was fairly good. The parents refused to consent, and the court sided with the parents in not approving treatment. The decision has received considerable criticism. For example, Andrew Bainham has argued that the case fails to distinguish between the interests of the parents and the interests of the child and gives undue weight to parents' rights and inadequate weight to the child's rights (Bainham 1997). But Jo

[82] [2017] EWHC 3619 (Fam).

[83] [1997] 1 WLR 242.

Bridgeman has argued that this is an unfair criticism (Bridgeman 2008, Chap. 1). Although the consultant team were unanimous that the surgery should go ahead, they disagreed on whether it was appropriate to go ahead *without the co-operation of parents*. Given the parental opposition there was not, therefore, clear agreement among the medical professionals that the procedure was in the best interests of the child. The medical procedure required the mother to be totally committed to caring for the child post-operatively and to return to the UK from overseas where she and her partner had taken up new jobs. The case is not, therefore a case in which parents' rights triumph over those of the child. Rather it acknowledges that relationship of care between the parent and child is central to the child's well-being (Herring 2014, Chap. 6).

1.6 Summary in Relation to Decision-Making on Behalf of Children

The legal test is the same as for incapacitous adults: what is in the best interests of the patient? And broadly the same principles have been used as in adult cases. But in relation to children, because the parent-child relationship is so obviously important, well-being has been expressed more explicitly in terms of relationality—an emphasis we endorse, and which we think could and should be exported into decision-making for incapacitous adults.

References

Bainham A (1997) Do babies have rights? Camb Law J 56:48
Bridgeman J (2008) Parents, young children and healthcare law. Cambridge University Press, Cambridge
Foster C (2012) Human dignity in bioethics and law. Hart, Oxford
Foster C, Herring J (2017) Identity, personhood, and the law. Springer, London
Herring J (2016) The welfare principle. Presumably it is about welfare. JSWFL
Herring J (2014) Caring and the law. Hart, Oxford

Chapter 2
The Idea of Human Thriving: A Brief History

Abstract This chapter examines the evolution of the notion of the Good Life, from the Upper Palaeolithic until modern times. It looks particularly at the ancient Greek and Roman worlds, the significance of the doctrine of the Imago Dei in Judaeo-Christian thought, the growing influence of autonomy from the Renaissance onwards, and the tension between utilitarianism and more individualistic models of human thriving.

Keywords Good life · Classical world · Judaeo-Christian · Mediaeval Renaissance · Enlightenment

2.1 Introduction

No doubt every human who has ever existed has had an idea about how best to live their life. Humans generally seek to avoid pain, to have shelter, and adequate food and fluids, and to live in communities. They change their environment so that it conforms more with their own idea of how life should be. They make clothes, they build dwellings, and they cook food.

At least from the Upper Palaeolithic onwards there are clear signs of consciousness: self-assertions in figurative form, indicating that the artist regards him or herself as an entity distinct from other individuals: assertions of subjectivity.[1] Parallel with these assertions there are indications (in grave goods and votive objects) of religious belief—of belief that human life is more than merely material. The same anti-mechanistic view of humans is embodied in increasingly elaborate decorative art: there are, from very early on, signs of dissatisfaction with the merely natural: pots, for some reason, are better if they are decorated; walls are better if they are painted.

[1]Most famously in the 'Venus of Brassempouy'—one of the first known representations of the human form: an ivory figurine from the Upper Palaeolithic, c 25,000 years old.

C. Foster and J. Herring, *Human Thriving and the Law*, SpringerBriefs in Law,
https://doi.org/10.1007/978-3-030-01135-2_2

But, so far as we know, systematic attempts to articulate what is meant by the Good Life are of relatively recent origin. This chapter surveys some of the main accounts.

A preliminary point: it is common to see secular accounts of the Good Life presented as antithetical to religious accounts. A good and strident example is A. C. Grayling:

> …mankind's quest for the good has been a struggle between humanism, on the one hand, and religious conceptions of the world, on the other hand…For six or seven centuries from the height of classical Athens to the last flourishing of the Antonine dynasty in Imperial Rome, thinking about the good life was premised on principles which….were fundamentally those of enlightenment and humanism, so nameable not just because they are the source of intellectual attitudes which bear those labels in later times (the Renaissance and the eighteenth-century Enlightenment), but because that is exactly what they were in themselves.
>
> Then, for a period more than twice as long, the Western world—for most of that time restricted to Europe—lay under the ideological hegemony of Christianity, which, although it adopted and adapted much from the ethical thought of classical antiquity, also flatly rejected most of its bases in favour of a quite different view, namely that the source of value lies outside the world, embodied in the commands and requirements of a personal deity (Grayling 2007, x, xii–xiii).

Many of the factual assertions in this passage are correct, but the dichotomy it sets up is false. While the Abrahamic religions may seem to locate the source of value outside the world, they claim that those values are necessary for human thriving because they relate directly to the way that human beings actually are. They have, in other words, an anthropology that is just as explicit, just as important in determining the content of ethical codes, and often very similar to, the anthropology assumed by secular humanism. The picture of man drawn by the Abrahamic religions is strikingly similar to that drawn by observant humanists. And accordingly there is a remarkable convergence of views about the central moral imperatives in all ages and in all cultures. Nobody, anywhere, has thought it commendable to be mean or dishonest. Everybody, everywhere, has applauded altruism. This, we think, is an indication that views of the good life, whether or not they appeal explicitly to a god or gods, only endure and are promulgated widely if they accord with the basic biological and sociological characteristics of human beings.

There are some apparent counter-examples—notably the current toxic movements of fundamentalist Christianity (particularly in the USA) and Islamism. We entirely accept that no right-thinking person would look at Westboro Baptist Church[2] and say: 'There is life in all its fullness.'[3] We suggest, though, that these are not counter-examples at all. Both are very recent and self-limiting movements.

---

[2]In Topeka, Kansas, noted for its 'God Hates Fags' campaigns.

[3]In John 10:10 Jesus, in a comment that endorses the idea of the Good Life, says that he has 'come that they may have life, and have it to the full.' (NIV).

White evangelicalism in the US is ageing and diminishing. Young people are haemorrhaging away from it fast.[4] And Islamism, while it has flared up periodically since the nineteenth century, shows no sign of becoming a mainstream movement.

2.2 Ideas of the Good Life in the Ancient Greek and Roman Worlds

Homer had his heroes, and they evinced heroic virtues such as courage and shrewdness. But they were far more concerned with how to die than with how to live. For them there was value in living a heroically virtuous life, but only because it would help to secure their reputation in posterity, and because the best way to ensure that one died a virtuous death was to be perpetually in a state of heroic virtue. One never knew when the final bronze sword would be inserted between your ribs. And, anyway, most humans were not heroes, and could not aspire to it. A hero was a hero as a result of divine favour, and the favour of the capricious gods and goddesses of Olympus could not be reliably bought. The duties, privileges and daily timetable of Achilles were very different from those of an ordinary Athenian —let alone an ordinary Spartan or Egyptian. One cannot conclude anything very meaningful about normative human thriving from the *Iliad.*

Of course this is not to say that there were no such normative assumptions in the Mycenaean Bronze Age. There plainly were. Although the principal characters in the *Iliad* and the Odyssey are heroes, the *Iliad* is the story of a war to recover an abducted queen (and thus, to some extent, a denunciation of abduction), and the *Odyssey* is a story about homecoming (and thus a celebration of home and of Penelope's faithfulness). Grayling says (talking mainly about the later Classical age and later) that 'Greeks had no sense of sin. They called moral failings *amartiai*, 'bad shots', the sort of things that can happen to anyone and are best put behind one, except as reminders to take better aim next time' (Grayling 2007, 12). This comment is misconceived, both in relation to the Classical and later periods, and in relation to the time from the Homeric to the Classical age. It is right that '*amartiai'* referred to bad shots—but this is exactly the sense in which St. Paul described sin: '…all have sinned and fall short of the glory of God'[5] and exactly the sense in which Judaism has traditionally described moral shortcomings. Only with Augustine's imaginative creation of the un-Biblical doctrine of original sin did 'sin' acquire the connotation that Grayling assumes is fundamental to the understanding of sin. The 'falling short' connotation did not mean that this type of sin was not serious. Look at the trouble and expense to which Greeks from the most ancient

[4]See, e.g., http://www.newsweek.com/trump-evangelicals-support-millennials-888267.

[5]Romans 3:23. '*Amartiai'* is not used there, but 'sinned' is expounded in terms that echo '*amartiai*'.

times went to appease the gods. This was not just a reflection of divine caprice: it was an expression of genuine concern that human actions inconsistent with some normative standard would have dire effects.

It is one thing to have a moral sense: almost all human beings do. It is another to have a moral philosophy.

It is not clear when the Greeks can first be said to have a moral philosophy. Some suggest that it is there in Homer: we have argued against that suggestion. Others would point to Protagoras' famous dictum, 'Man is the measure of all things', and suggest that this is prototypic humanism—making human characteristics and demands the yardsticks determining moral conduct. But it is hard to read so much into this obscure observation. It could equally be a statement that the universe exists for the benefit of humans, or that the physical characteristics of humans are reflected in the physical design of the world.

Was Socrates the first Greek moral philosopher? That is too big a claim. Perhaps the most that can be said is that he was the first to declare that the question of how we should live is not only an important matter of philosophical enquiry, but also a more important, urgent, and fruitful area of enquiry than the nature of the physical world—which had previously been the main concern of Greek philosophers.

The zeal with which Socrates (and Plato[6]) insisted that it matters how we spend our lives, and matters how we think about how we spend our lives, was partly a reaction to their disgust at the Sophists—intellectual prostitutes: brains for hire—who would turn their talents to any cause. This wasn't acceptable, said Socrates and Plato: it prompted them to defend the idea of the *normative*—in Plato's case to the extent of his promulgation of the doctrine of the Forms, whereby there is a normative realm, inhabited by the types or forms of everyday things and phenomena, and to which we should try to approximate. Plato locates morality in these Forms—though very generally.

But neither Socrates nor Plato prescribe any real content for the normative demands that they insist are important. We should work at perfecting our souls, says Socrates, and in order to do so we need to acquire knowledge of the value of things. But he is silent about what this entails. Dogmatically so: he is applauded by the Delphic oracle for admitting that he knows nothing.

While Plato appeals to the Forms as the ultimate source of value, he never spells out in any detail what this means for our living other than (in teaching that preshadows Aristotle's Golden Mean and the notion of *Eudaemonia*) that our souls should keep in balance our rationality, our emotions, and our appetites.[7]

---

[6]Book 1 of the *Republic* contains some virulent diatribes against the Sophists.

[7]Plato gave a lecture entitled 'On the Good'. It was apparently very disappointing. Aristoxenus of Tarentum explains: '*Each came expecting to learn something about the things that are generally considered good for men, such as wealth, good health, physical strength, and altogether a kind of wonderful happiness. But when the mathematical demonstrations came, including numbers, geometrical figures and astronomy, and finally the statement Good is One seemed to them, I imagine, utterly unexpected and strange; hence some belittled the matter, while others rejected it.*'

The first known attempt to set out the reasons why we should live in a particular way, combined with the first attempt to specify the conduct implied by those reasons, was Aristotle's *Nichomachean Ethics*. It is the high point of philosophical naturalism, for it asserts that the way that we in fact are, and the way that we naturally think, are the keys to the ways that we *should* live. Anthropology leads moral philosophy: we can (heretical though it is for modern philosophers), infer *ought* from *is*. For Aristotle, it matters that we are happy: this fact means that happiness itself is a good. Because we are the sorts of creatures that we are, we will, if we're properly calibrated, desire that good. This good is not in another realm: it is ascertainable and attainable now, and if we use our reason properly we will strive to ascertain and attain it. Reasoning is the quintessential human activity. The proper exercise of our reason will lead us to acquire the Good that is concordant with our human nature. Reason, properly exercised, is therefore a *humanizing* activity.

What will our reason show us? That virtue—and hence the happiness of balance —of *eudaimonia*—lies in the middle way between undesirable extremes. Behave this way and you will have *eudaimonia*: your soul will swell: you will be more normatively human.

For most of us, this project cannot be undertaken alone. There may be a few, ultra-elite contemplatives, but generally (it is, after all, an application of the Golden Mean) we should avoid both crowds and solitude: our nature decrees that *eudaimonia* cannot be attained in a mountain eyrie: we are social animals. Rational, eudaemonic relationship implies altruism and civic responsibility.

Although Socrates and Plato were not explicit about the nature of happiness or the demands of virtue, they certainly saw themselves as social animals with civic responsibilities. Although *The Republic* is more concerned with metaphysics than politics, the very fact that it is framed as it is (as a picture of the ideal community, in which *society* is better if it listens to the philosophers who are in touch with the knowledge that makes virtue and good living possible) indicates Plato's assumption that thriving humans are socially embedded humans. This assumption is made explicit in Aristotle.

This was perhaps a consequence of the fact that Socrates, Plato, and Aristotle knew that what they thought and said and wrote *mattered*:[8] it had social and political consequences. They lived in small aristocratic communities: they influenced the *zeitgeist*, and could see that they did.

The philosophers of the Hellenistic world could not maintain such a conceit. Alexander's empire was a vast, decentralized, unwieldy entity. The old city states of the Athenian Golden Age lost much of their importance. What the philosophers said in their salons did not have so immediately obvious an effect on the way that people thought, felt, and lived. The result was a sort of pietism: philosophy (and

---

Elementa harmonica II: 30–31, cited Gaiser, Konrad (1980). 'Plato's enigmatic lecture: 'On the Good'' Phronesis 25(1); 5–37.

[8]In *The Republic*, Book 10, Plato suggests that all of Homer's works should be banned, because Homer has never achieved anything useful or made anyone virtuous.

particularly conceptions of the Good Life) became more intimately personal concerns (and concomitantly less *social* concerns) than they had been. One might say that they were more expressly concerned with *self*-determination than (as the old philosophies had been) with social policy. But it is probably more accurate to say that the conception of the self had changed. In the time of Socrates, Plato, and Aristotle the self could only be defined in relation to the society in which it was embedded: the boundaries of the self were porous. The self became more of an atomistic entity in the Hellenistic age: the boundaries of the self hardened.

The philosophies of this age seem modern. The Cynics railed in a dreadlocked way against the strictures of the conventional conservatives. Freedom was their watchword. They showed their contempt for the mores of the suburbs by refusing to wash, by wearing ragged or no clothes, by advocating a radical simplicity and contempt for material goods, and by repudiating ancient taboos such as incest. Diogenes, the architect of Cynicism (if one can have an architect of an anti-architectural, anarchistic movement) famously masturbated in public. For the Cynic (echoing Hinduism and Buddhism), suffering came from attachment to vanities—such as possessions. Release the attachment, and suffering would evaporate.

Cynicism (in this sense) has never gone away. It has usefully and effectively interrogated the self-satisfied assumptions of successive empires. But it is essentially a negative philosophy: a reaction to conservatism and thus a creature of conservatism. It is hardly creative, and its picture of humans and their needs is too simple for it ever to satisfy by itself for very long. There is more to human thriving than simply to do what you feel like, when you feel like it.

There was more substance to Epicureanism. It has acquired an unfortunate reputation. Yes, it was concerned with the pursuit of pleasure and the avoidance of pain, but what it meant by pleasure was far removed from the Bacchanalian orgies often associated with the adjective ‘Epicurean’. It perceived that the good life was best approached by simplicity; by placing a high value on friendship, and by breaking the hold that material things and death itself have on us. God, said the Epicureans, would not judge us. He was not very interested in the world at all—and certainly not interested in us personally. Death simply entailed the dispersion of our component parts. We could not experience angst about our pre-birth non-existence, and hence it was non-sensical to fear our post-mortem non-existence.

Epicureanism, like Cynicism, feels very contemporary. Yet, like Epicureanism, it is best characterised not as a philosophy, but as a refusal to philosophise. It embodied a low view of human life which does not resonate with our own intuitions about the significance of our own lives and those of others, and it side-stepped the problem of suffering.

These criticisms cannot be levelled at the third great philosophical movement of the Hellenistic world—Stoicism. Neither Cynicism nor Epicureanism has gone away, but their influence—at least on serious thinkers—pales into insignificance beside that of Stoicism. Stoicism has endured and has been massively influential. There is one main reason, and two subsidiary reasons. The main reason is that it is an unapologetically naturalistic philosophy. It purports to derive the rules of human conduct and the criteria for human thriving from the way that the world is. To live well is to live naturally. The two subsidiary (and related) reasons are, first, that it started with a search for the most fundamental principle governing the way that things (including human beings) are. If one starts from fundamental principles one is more likely (if the search is successful) to generate solutions that do not crumble. And, second, Stoicism did not dodge the hard questions—notably of death and suffering: it took the philosophical bull by the horns.

There was, said the Stoics, a coherent principle underpinning everything in the universe: the *logos.* Early Stoics identified the *logos* with Zeus: John's Gospel asserts that Jesus is the divine *logos.* Since the *logos* permeates everything and everyone, it is to some degree accessible to everyone. There is a deep democracy at the heart of Stoicism—a democracy akin to the Jewish notion of the *Imago Dei.* Very unlike the Homeric world, where gifts were handed out by the gods and goddesses to their chosen few, all could appropriate the *logos* and all should aspire to do so. The duty to be good—a duty owed to oneself and to the rest of the world —was a duty to work to align ones life and thought with the *logos.* A Good Life was one lived in alignment with it.

The *logos* was itself Good, and accordingly, if one lived a properly natural life, there was nothing to fear: neither suffering nor death would touch the composure of the truly natural man.

If the *logos* permeates and actuates all, one's view of the Self, and of other humans, and of nature, and of the demands of virtue, will necessarily be communitarian. We are all intimately related to everyone and everything else.

Communitarianism, then, vague in Socrates and Plato, explicit in Aristotle, absent in Cynicism, diluted in Epicureanism, was recovered and put centre stage in Stoicism.

Stoicism (and particularly this communitarian aspect) was influential throughout much of the Roman period (notably in the writings of Marcus Aurelius). It is interesting to reflect on the fact that the Romans (militaristic triumphalists if ever there were militaristic triumphalists) adopted as one of their foundation myths the story of the Trojans. For the Trojans lost. Troy was destroyed. Why choose a loser as your mythological forbear, when you could choose a winner? Grayling shrewdly suggests that Hector (who fought not for himself but for Troy, and was thinking about the safety of his wife and family when he strode out to clash with Achilles), and Aeneas (who stumbled out of the blazing city leading his son by the hand, and carrying his father on his back) better reflected Roman civic virtues and the corporate Roman sense of identity than the flat, icy, self-possessed and self-obsessed Greeks.[9]

---

[9]Ibid, p. 20.

2.3 Ideas of the Good Life in the Jewish and Christian Worlds

Happiness, in one form or another, features prominently in most Greek and Roman accounts of human thriving. But while the Hebrew Bible and Jewish commentaries have a great deal to say about happiness, happiness is never, in either Judaism or Christianity, an objective in its own right. 'Judaism', says the former Chief Rabbi Jonathan Sacks, is concerned with 'life, liberty, and the pursuit of *holiness.*'[10] This is shrewd. As we will see when we examine the empirical literature on what constitutes happiness, if we aim at happiness, we will generally miss it. If we aim at something else worthy (and notably if we aim at the happiness of others), happiness is likely to be a by-product. In the *Guide to the Perplexed*, Maimonides summarises accurately the gist of the modern findings: someone who does what is right because it is right will find that happiness comes.[11]

There is, in any event, no one form of happiness in Judaism. The first word of the first verse of Psalm 1 is the Hebrew word *ashrei*—often rendered as 'happy'. But *ashrei* is a *plural* construct, best translated along the lines of 'these are the happinesses of…'[12]

Sacks identifies three basic ways in which Judaism understands happiness. The first is the happiness that comes from struggle; from taking part in something worthwhile. Note that the name 'Israel' was the name given to Jacob after he had wrestled with the angel.[13] It means 'He who contends with God'. Contending with God, therefore, is the defining characteristic of the Jewish people.

'The Sages have no rest', says the Talmud, 'either in this world or the next'. And indeed many great Biblical heroes, far from smiling their way blithely through life, asked to die. Think of Moses, Elijah, Jeremiah, Jonah, and Job. The Jewish commission, says Sacks, is a commission of active engagement with the world, driven by the 'cognitive dissonance between the world as it is and the world as it ought to be.' That sort of drivenness is not what we usually think of as happiness—and it is certainly a long way from the blissful, detached calm often held up by eastern religions as the ideal human state. And yet there is a sort of happiness—a sort of calm—that can come only from participation in the melee of existence. Abraham, Sacks points out, had a life of terrific turbulence. He was uprooted from his family home in Mesopotamia, travelled across the Middle East where, in the land he had been promised, he found only famine. He left the promised land and travelled to Egypt, where he had to pass off his wife, Sarah, as his sister. He had been promised a great multitude of children, but he was an old man before he had even one. When Sarah died, despite the divine promise of a vast territory, he,

[10]*Happiness in the Jewish Perspective,* lecture at the Center for the Study of Law and Religion, Emory University, 2010.

[11]Chapter 11: cited Sacks, ibid.

[12]Sacks, ibid.

[13]Genesis 32: 22–32.

owning no land at all, had to buy land at an inflated price in order to bury her. And yet, at the end of his life, the Bible says that he died at a great old age, satisfied with life.

Sacks' second category of Jewish happiness is the happiness described in the Wisdom literature—a sort of happiness akin to that described by the Greeks and the eastern traditions: a happiness associated with balance and virtue. It is exemplified by Psalm 1: the man who delights in the law of the Lord, and meditates on that law, and who 'walks not in the counsel of the ungodly, nor stands in the path of sinners, nor sits in the seat of the scornful, is like a tree which brings forth fruit in its season. Whatever he does prospers. It is a picture of rootedness; of fecundity. The man who is happy in this sense is contrasted with the ungodly man who is blown by the wind; rich soil is contrasted with sand.

Sacks' third category is 'social happiness'. This may seem to be in tension with the supreme importance attached to the individual by the notion of the Imago Dei, but the book of Genesis, after noting all the good things about the creation, asserts that it is *not good* for humans to be alone.[14] That, as we will see, tallies well with the empirical evidence. In the Jewish mainstream there is an emphatic rejection of seclusion. Apart from the Qumran sect, there are no Jewish monasteries, and celibacy is frowned upon. Happiness of this sort is to be found in relationship; in community; in the family. It is, in the broadest sense of the word, *political* happiness.

A related idea, again highlighted by Sacks, is the Jewish insistence on the importance of the material; on the primacy of health and well-being. Judaism rejects rejection. It has—in the mainstream—no tradition of asceticism. Poverty is an evil. In the *Guide to the Perplexed* Maimonides, talking about the perfection of the body and the perfection of the soul, says that the perfection of the body is the priority, because one cannot think noble thoughts if one is in dire physical straits. There is a very illuminating rabbinic commentary on the Nazirites—the nearest that the Hebrew Bible gets to holy mendicants. Nazirites take a vow not to drink wine and not to cut their hair.[15] When they end their period as a Nazirite, and return to ordinary life, they have to bring a sin offering. Why? The intuitive answer (to minds used to the ascetic tradition in Christianity) is that the offering is needed to atone for the sin of ceasing to be a Nazirite, and immersing oneself again in more secular life. But the rabbis' answer was exactly the opposite: it was needed to atone for the sin of becoming a Nazirite in the first place, since to be a Nazirite involved repudiation of, inter alia, the divine gift of wine.[16]

---

[14]Genesis 2: 18.

[15]See Numbers 6:1–11.

[16]See Talmud Nazir 22a: '*As it is taught in a baraita that Rabbi Elazar HaKappar the esteemed says: What is the meaning when the verse states: 'And make atonement for him, for that he sinned by reason of the soul' (Numbers 6:11)? And with which soul did this nazirite sin? Rather, because he deprived himself of wine he is therefore called a sinner. And are not these matters inferred a fortiori: And if this one, who deprived himself only of wine, is nevertheless called a sinner, in the case of one who deprives himself of everything by fasting or other acts of mortification, all the more so is he labeled a sinner.*

The Jewish picture of thriving, then, is one in which happiness is not to be aimed at: there are other priorities. Happiness can only ever be a by-product of an effort to be virtuous—in the sense of seeking to keep the law and seeking the good of others rather than oneself. Happiness, when it comes, emerges more often than not from struggle; from a working out of the imperative to transform the world; to make virtue increase; to realise the messianic ideal and to bring the world into the just place spoken of by the prophets who raged against the abuse of power and the marginalisation of the weak. Though the primary picture is of happiness in the eye of the storm, there is a subsidiary picture—of fruit-bearing as a result of rootedness. Where this happens it converges with the notion of contentment. Whichever type of happiness is realised, it can only be realised properly in community. And thriving—though it is likely to entail proper spiritual orientation—is maximised by physical integrity and by an appreciation of human embodiedness.

It is worth pointing out, too, not only that Judaism presupposes a clear connection between virtue and thriving (Psalm 1 makes the point well), but is also far more explicit than any of the Greeks about what virtue entails. The Ten Commandments are clear; so are the laws of *halakhah;* and so are the seven Noahide laws, said to be obligatory for non-Jews. In these stipulations there is none of the room for negotiation and argument inherent in, for instance, Aristotle's formulation of the Golden Mean.

Although some nuances of this Jewish view of human thriving were worked out after the birth of Christianity, to a first degree of approximation this was the view inherited by early Christianity. Christianity, of course, had at its core an urgency that Judaism did not have. Christians believed that Jesus was, if not God, then at least the long expected Messiah who would put the world's wrongs to right and establish the conditions necessary for the whole world to thrive; who would establish justice and righteousness. Swords would be beaten into ploughshares, wars would end, and the wolf would lie down with the lamb. The resurrection of Jesus was a sure sign of his messiahship. After the ascension there was no immediate institution of the messianic age, but that would come. Jesus had promised that he was coming again soon—within the lifetime of some of those listening to his prophecy—and when he did the world would be transformed.

St Paul believed that the messianic age was about to be ushered in. That was the context of his lack of interest in many of the traditional areas of Jewish concern—notably the family. He famously urged the unmarried not to marry.[17] This was not because he had abandoned the Jewish conviction that marriage and families were important, but because he thought that the imminent second coming of Jesus meant that it was pointless to invest time and effort in anything temporal. Similar observations apply to his direction to have respect—for the time being—for secular authorities. It simply didn't matter much, he thought, whether you married or

According to this opinion, she brings a sin-offering to atone for uttering the vow itself, despite the fact that her husband later uprooted it entirely.'

[17]1 Corinthians 7:1; 7: 8–9.

whether you nodded to a repressive regime: neither marriage nor the regime were going to be around for much longer.

Both Jesus and Paul were wrong. Jesus did not return. Very gradually the mainstream church came to terms with the fact that the world as we know it is likely to persist for a while. Two thousand years later some Christians have still failed to do so.

The early church fought many battles for its survival. One of the most important battles, which determined the shape of Christian doctrine, was against Gnosticism. Gnosticism took many forms. The significant aspect of its (very varied) theology for present purposes was its denigration of the material; of bodies; of the here and now. What mattered was the spiritual. It forged predictable and powerful alliances with Platonists: the doctrine of the Forms mapped well onto many Gnostic ideas. And, though they would have denied the influence, the early Christian ascetics who meditated in desert caves and on the top of pillars had a good deal in common with the Gnostics too.

The Christians responded to the challenge by asserting that matter mattered. They emphasised and promoted those parts of the Gospels that insisted that the resurrection body of Jesus ate kippers, promulgated creeds that said that Jesus was fully human as well as fully God, and, consistent with its Jewish roots, had no time for sacerdotal celibacy.

Augustine of Hippo[18] caused the western church to relinquish much of the ground won in its battle against the Gnostics. He had been a Manichaean, and never really gave up Manichaeism. He was profoundly influenced by Platonism, and had a personal distaste for sex which he theologised into the doctrine of Original Sin, unknown to the Bible or to Jewish tradition, which held that sin was a sexually transmitted infection.

This had enormously repercussive and lasting effects on the western church's view of human thriving (the eastern church, despite its rapport with Plato, was and is suspicious of Augustine). Humans, on Augustine's view, were contaminated from birth; they were wretches whose capacity to do good or think good was severely truncated. Augustine rewrote the doctrine of the *Imago Dei.* More obvious in humans was the *Imago tartari.*[19] This view of humans dominates modern Protestant (and particularly evangelical) views of the potential of human reason.

Augustine's denigration of the body represented a tectonic shift from Jewish tradition. Ascetics came to be seen as the church's elite; celibacy was a virtue, and celibates were the legislators. But there were more subtle and far-reaching effects. The most important characteristics of humans were perceived as being *spiritual* attributes. Real, lasting worth lay not in anything that could be achieved in this world, but what was being accumulated in a spiritual realm. Such a move was understandable in the rhetoric of St. Paul, who every day expected history to come to an end. It was less excusable four hundred years from the death and non-return of

[18]354-430 CE.

[19]Thanks to Sally Foster for this expression.

Jesus. It had the effect of elevating abstraction over the concrete; of raising the general over the particular. Plato had triumphed.

Any account of human thriving that posits that intangible spiritual qualities are the only ones worth taking into account is likely to fall short. Such an account will facilitate frightening abuses. If someone's eternal destiny can be assured by forcible conversion, or his eternal life improved by temporal torture, is there not a moral imperative to prepare the rack or the tongs? And apparently immoral omissions will be justified: why feed the hungry when their heavenly life matters so much more than their earthly life—and when, indeed, their temporal suffering might be, from an eternal perspective, a shrewd investment? It encouraged a view of humans as abstractions. If humans really were inhabitants of heaven rather than here, why bother to study them in their earthly habitat to establish how they might best live here? The real nature of man was to be established by reference to scripture (or to Augustine's spin on scripture), not by reference to data. Human views about what constituted human thriving were necessarily suspect—twisted by the Fall; clouded by fleshly appetite. There was a war (foreshadowed by Plato, who had talked about the horse of physical appetite dragging the chariot of the soul away from the direction chosen by the charioteer, reason) between the spirit and the flesh. Or, put another way, humans were the battlegrounds in which principalities and powers waged their war. What mattered was the outcome of the war, not the damage that was done to the battlefield.

By the time that the Dark Ages swept in from the east and the north, western Christianity had adopted a pastiche both of the Jewish world views of Jesus and Paul, and of the nature of humans. Eastern Christianity remained relatively Jewish, but was increasingly incarcerated behind high political walls, and had very limited ability to mitigate either the damage done by the Platonisation of the west or to influence the renaissance that occurred in the fourteenth century.

The love of abstraction which had its roots in Plato, the Gnostics, and Augustine had its full flowering in mediaeval Scholasticism. Its literature is noted for earnest debates and dogmatic assertions about invisible entities, and for its almost complete lack of interest in matter.

2.4 Ideas of the Good Life in the Renaissance and the Enlightenment

The Renaissance was a rediscovery of particularity; of the concrete; of the immediate; of the natural. It was a movement characterised by a suspicion of the abstractions that had held the mediaeval mind in thrall. Its art celebrated the natural world and the physicality of the human form. It drew strength from the newly disinterred classics of the ancient Mediterranean world—and particularly from Stoicism. Stoicism's philosophic naturalism legitimized the process (articulated by Aristotle) of drawing conclusions about the way humans should live from conclusions about the type of creatures humans are and the characteristics of the world in which they live.

One of the results of this concern with particularity was a focus on *individual* humans. Recall that in Jewish philosophy there was a tension between the notion of the individual human's immense (indeed divine) worth (as expressed in the doctrine of the *Imago Dei*) and the conviction that individuals were crucially social animals, who could not function properly outside a community. That vital tension was forgotten by the Renaissance humanists in their excited rediscovery of the value of the individual.

This amnesia was abetted by the prominence of Stoicism in the humanist revolution. As we have seen, Stoicism believed that, since the *logos* permeated all, it was at least desirable to seek to live in accordance with the dictates of the *logos*. This had consequences for all human actions and omissions. It enthroned human reason, for human reason could discern and should respond to the *logos*. It followed that human X had an obligation to behave in line with the *logos* which was independent of what human Y might decide to do or not to do. This view of individual moral responsibility spawned a new model of human identity. Humans were atomistic entities, rather like billiard balls. The boundaries between individual humans were hard and impervious. A curious process was at work: the idea of a *logos* (of unspecified nature) had created a model of human identity which in turn dictated the nature of the *logos* that had created it. The child determined the characteristics of its parent. The new *logos* of the Renaissance was autonomy: self rule—a notion that of course implies (we say implausibly) that it is possible to give a single, accurate account of any individual 'self'. Pico della Mirandola[20] put it like this: 'Oh wondrous and unsurpassable felicity of man, to whom it is granted to have what he chooses, to be what he wills to be!'[21]

Scholasticism took a long time to dissolve. Indeed its core assumptions about the source of value and the relative unimportance of the material seeped into Reformation theology and persist there to this day. But Europe was never the same again. The Reformation itself adopted the Renaissance humanists' view of individual (as opposed to corporate) responsibility. What was important in determining one's own eternal destiny was one's own personal response to God, rather than the fact that one was grafted into the body of the Church. Noah's Ark (a crowded vessel of salvation) was replaced by tiny, individually piloted boats. And (contrary to what Jesus had clearly and repeatedly taught) it was not primarily one's *acts* that mattered. Salvation was by faith, and faith was a mental position. If you *thought* the right things about God, you would be safe. This raised mental states to a status they had never previously had, and similarly demoted the community of faith.

We have already criticised Grayling's view of the history of human thriving. He sees that history as characterised by perpetual tension between the transcendental and the material[22]; between religion and secularism; between divine tyranny and

[20] 1463-94. He was himself an enthusiastic Neo-Platonist, profoundly influenced by Kabbalah.

[21] *Oration on the Dignity of Man*, 1486.

[22] 'The quest for the good has, in all epochs, primarily taken the form of conflict between humanistic and transcendentalist perspectives': Grayling, ibid, p 132.

humanistic freedom. That view is, we suggest, very plainly wrong until the Enlightenment. But as a summary of the position from the Enlightenment to the present day it is broadly and tragically true. The Enlightenment saw itself, narcissistically, as a bold break from the prison of superstition, with anti-clerical activists such as Voltaire leading the charge. Movements of reaction (and the Enlightenment was a textbook example of reaction) are rarely characterised by nuance; their script is dictated by their opponent, and the result tends to be slogan and sclerosis.

The Enlightenment was concerned to rehabilitate humans; it did so by demoting God. Nothing, in principle, was inaccessible to human reason, and that meant that mystery was illegitimate. Mystery, after all, had so often been the category to which the church had appealed in order to avoid interrogation by human reason. The result was a new religion: a religion of reason. Science, which is a *method*, mutated into a *metaphysics*. Just like the old religion of Christianity, it had its creeds, and hence it has, and has, its Inquisitions, thumbscrews, and heretics. The cosmos, for the Enlightenment thinker, was a machine. Machines were predictable and perfectly describable. They also have no souls. The natural world, which had previously been seen as an archipelago of ensouled creatures, was now a cabinet of curiosities made merely of matter. This evolved into the dictum that minds are brains, and therefore do not extend beyond skulls—so reducing very significantly the capacity for inchoate relationship. And it paved the way, too, for the exploitation of the natural world. There is nothing immoral about destroying a machine. It does not entail the destruction of an ensouled creature.[23]

The Renaissance and Enlightenment were times of genuinely spectacular advances in the natural and mechanistic sciences, but their guiding philosophers had specifically eschewed the constraints necessary to prevent the advances from becoming (in terms of human thriving) retreats; from preventing the machines from becoming masters. The Enlightenment spawned the Industrial Revolution, and the Industrial Revolution poisoned and enslaved.

To enshrine human reason was necessarily to insist on individual responsibility (as Stoicism and, for rather different reasons, the Reformation, had done). It also (and this was not necessary) presumed an atomistic view of the individual.

---

[23]The seeds of this revolution had been sown in the 17th century by Descartes (1596–1650) and Hobbes (1588–1679). Descartes' crucial move was to divide the universe into two distinct parts: the immaterial (into which he placed human minds and 'spiritual' entities) and matter. It seems innocent. But it entails an assertion that matter has no mind. Bodies—both human and animal—were quietly but emphatically demoted. They had previously been seen as infused by spirit. Now they were machines. For Hobbes, the state in which humans would exist without a social contract was wretched: '*there is no place for industry; because the fruit thereof is uncertain: and consequently no culture of the earth; no navigation, nor use of the commodities that may be imported by sea; no commodious building; no instruments of moving, and removing, such things as require much force; no knowledge of the face of the earth; no account of time; no arts; no letters; no society; and which is worst of all, continual fear, and danger of violent death; and the life of man, solitary, poor, nasty, brutish, and short*'. (*Leviathan*, 1651). To thrive, then, was to escape from this state of nature.

'Early modern men and women did think that life should have a purpose', observes David Wootton. 'Aristotle had told them so. Where, increasingly, they differed from Aristotle was in thinking that any purpose would do….[A] small linguistic change marks the break-point [in the mid-17th century, when people stopped talking about one *summum bonum*]….people stopped talking about felicity, and began to talk about happiness.'[24] There was a new cult of self-realization, a new model of the self, and a new, relativistic, theory of value.

Yet the idea of an absolute good did not go quietly. It regrouped under the new banner of individualism, and held on for a while. Both Stoicism and the individualistic pietism of the Reformation, were reflected in the Enlightenment's most prominent and influential thinker, Emmanuel Kant.[25] All humans, he held, had dignity because they were reasoning creatures. It followed that they had a duty to use their reason. How should they use it? 'Act only according to that maxim whereby you can, at the same time, will that it should become a universal law' (Kant 1785, 39). This was the 'categorical imperative', and Kant used it to derive a number of specific moral injunctions.[26]

To thrive, for Kant, was to live in accordance with the *logos* that decreed the principle of the categorical imperative and the particular conclusion in specified cases of the categorical imperative. His is a lonely, elitist, isolationist creed, irrelevant in cases where the ability to reason is truncated (which of course includes many of the most important cases in medical ethics). 'Have courage to use your own understanding', he urged. It is hard to imagine a moral or intellectual injunction more prone to objection. Even if all the objections can be met in relation to people with normal cognition (and they cannot), Kant would seem to have no way of saying that a seriously brain damaged patient is thriving—however much apparent pleasure the patient has or gives.

The scepticism of transcendentalism that had characterised the more brash rhetoric of the Enlightenment had its most explicit philosophical expression in the work of the Scottish philosopher David Hume.[27] Yet Hume is far too subtle and prolific a thinker to fit neatly into any of the established philosophical categories. We suspect that he would be shocked to find his name used to endorse the

---

[24]'Desire without end': Times Literary Supplement, 27 February 2009, p. 3.

[25]1724–1804.

[26]For instance, re the morality of suicide, he held that: '*A man reduced to despair by a series of misfortunes feels sick of life, but is still so far in possession of his reason that he can ask himself whether taking his own life would not be contrary to his duty to himself. Now he asks whether the maxim of his action could become a universal law of nature. But his maxim is this: from self-love I make as my principle to shorten my life when its continued duration threatens more evil than it promises satisfaction. There only remains the question as to whether this principle of self-love can become a universal law of nature. One sees at once that a contradiction in a system of nature whose law would destroy life by means of the very same feeling that acts so as to stimulate the furtherance of life, and hence there could be no existence as a system of nature. Therefore, such a maxim cannot possibly hold as a universal law of nature and is, consequently, wholly opposed to the supreme principle of all duty.*' Ibid., 30–31.

[27]1711–1776.

quasi-religious worship of the material reductionist paradigm commonly said to be the legacy of the Enlightenment.

Hume was a critic of transcendentalism primarily in the sense that he thought that one should start a process of reasoning with the least controversial—and hence most observable—types of evidence. 'Even Mathematics, Natural Philosophy, and Natural Religion, are, in some measure dependent on the science of man', he wrote, in *A Treatise of Human Nature* (1740). He was, therefore, a 'bottom-up' empiricist philosopher and a rigorously attentive epistemologist, attempting, in his work on ethics, to accommodate the facts of human psychology and physiology, and to take account of the biases inherent in our human constitution. This accommodation did not imply that he thought that one could derive absolute moral injunctions from nature (or that such injunctions existed). To the contrary: one of his most influential philosophical creations was the doctrine of the 'naturalistic fallacy'—the 'is-ought gap'—which asserts that it is illegitimate to derive an 'ought' from an 'is'.

Many of his conclusions are startlingly modern. He wrote, for instance: 'Morals excite passions, and produce or prevent actions. Reason of itself is utterly impotent in this particular. The rules of morality, therefore, are not conclusions of our reason.'[28] We will see precisely the same conclusion when we come, in Chap. 3, to examine the work of the contemporary scholar Jonathan Haidt.

We are not so much concerned with Hume's conclusions about human thriving. Indeed it is not clear what those conclusions are. Our main interest here is in his method—which we endorse completely. It illustrates what the Enlightenment could have been had it not deteriorated into anti-transcendental slogan and schism. He strove to reconcile Aristotle's insights about virtue ethics (with which he seems broadly to have agreed), with the facts that the Renaissance and Enlightenment's revelations about the nature of nature. For Hume it was nonsensical to talk about moral facts. But that did not mean it was nonsensical to observe that all societies agree that there are some virtues—and that there is substantial agreement about the identity of many of those virtues. For our purposes the ultimate source of those virtues (whether God, a Platonic realm, or evolutionarily ordained imperatives) does not matter.

There was a resistance at the time to the more strident contentions of the Enlightenment—contentions exemplified by Voltaire[29] and Kant—but the central Enlightenment theses (about the essentially mechanical nature of the Cosmos and of humans themselves, and of the sufficiency of individual human reason, and thus the centrality of the individual) carried the day in the realm of politics and economics. The resistance was an improbable coalition of reactionaries (who would have resisted any change, simply because it was change, and saw the anti-clericalism of the Enlightenment as apocalyptic) and romantics. The romantics are more interesting and significant than the reactionaries. Their central belief (which was taken up later by John Stuart Mill, and is increasingly voiced today), is that there is more

[28] *Treatise of Human Nature.*
[29] 1649–1722.

to the world, and particularly to humans, than that described by the material reductionism of Enlightenment thought. They were, in a sense, more humanist than the humanists, for they believed that humans were immensely complex creatures whose satisfaction demanded much more than food and sex. That satisfaction required too a relationship of a vibrant conversational kind with the non-human world. This insistence took the form, in some romantic discourse, of a return to the animism that had been the norm for most of human history. Others were less extreme. We will see, when we come to the empirical literature on human happiness, that the romantics have been fairly fully vindicated. They were, however, very much a guerrilla group in the 18th, 19th, and early 20th centuries.

In societies such as that of Periclean Athens, the connection between activity in the academy and the business of government was clear and direct: the thinkers were the rulers, or were on dining terms with them. But in modern times the connection (if any) is far harder to trace. The intellectual origins of the French Revolution (1789–1799) for instance, are much debated. Certainly the anti-clericalism of the Enlightenment played a part, as did the recognition of the rights of all men (which had its origins in the *Imago Dei*, but which had been forgotten in the Church-sponsored feudalism of the Middle Ages and had been rediscovered and secularised in the Renaissance and Enlightenment). But more than this it is hard to say. It *can* be argued that one can and should derive '*Liberté, egalité, fraternité*' from the view of human thriving that emerges from the Enlightenment. But it is not clear that this is correct. Political movements condition professional thinkers in the modern era probably far more than professional thinkers condition political movements. The French Revolution kindled much progressive thought on both sides of the Atlantic and the Channel, but the thought may have been spawned by the slogans of the Revolution rather than by the systematic thought that (perhaps) underpinned the Revolution.

2.5 From the Enlightenment to the Present

The 18th century ended and the 19th century began with a curious movement in the ascendant: utilitarianism. Its main pioneer was Jeremy Bentham.[30] It was (and is) curious because it combines two arguably conflicting assumptions: the assumption that individual concerns are the cornerstone of morality, and the assumption that moral behaviour entails subsuming individual concerns into considerations of the common good. Bentham wanted to maximise human happiness. When considering which of (say) two particular courses of action is justified one should, according to him, add up the effect of each action on the happiness (however defined) of the individual components of a society. The morally mandated action will be that which gives the greatest happiness to the greatest number.

[30] 1747–1832.

The communitarian focus of this 'felicific calculus' signalled a return to the ancient Athenian assumption that the 'good' should be defined in public terms. But what data did Bentham insist should be fed into his equation? Data about the good of individuals with hard boundaries, whose interests are likely to be determined without reference to the common good. It is not obvious that this is not an incoherent way to proceed.

This debate matters, for (although few would subscribe to strictly Benthamite ways of assessing the good of the greatest number), utilitarianism in one form or another continues to have a dominant place in the academy and an unassailable place in public policy.

Bentham had a defining influence on John Stuart Mill[31]—a more mature and less algorithmic thinker who had been salvaged from depression by Wordsworth and other romantic nature mystics. Mill's utilitarianism acknowledged (as Hume had done before him) that human happiness is a multi-faceted phenomenon. Mill sounds now like a metropolitan elitist, which (like all liberals then and most liberals now) he was. For him, not all pleasures were equal: there was a distinct hierarchy. And although he tends to speak in terms of pleasures, there is a clear overlap with virtues—and with the long tradition of virtue ethics. A properly directed mind will aim at the higher pleasures, and the central element of the good life is the possession of the freedom to cultivate the mind that will opt for the good. This has obvious political corollaries, and led to the promulgation of his famous 'harm principle': 'The only purpose for which power can be rightfully exercised over any member of a civilized community, against his will, is to prevent harm to others. His own good, either physical or moral, is not a sufficient warrant. He cannot rightfully be compelled to do or to forbear because it will be better for him to do so, because it will make him happier, because, in the opinions of others, to do so would be wise, or even right.'[32]

Modern reductionists tend to invoke and celebrate Hume and Mill. Yet it is hard to see modern reductionism as anything other than a pastiche of both—and indeed of the Renaissance origins of the Enlightenment. Hume was genuinely, sceptically scientific in a way that scientism is not. Mill was tortured, humane, and gave a priority to 'high' culture in a way that the technocratic 21st century does not. As so often, the original texts of the high priests are not read: bowdlerized versions have taken their place.

The mechanization of nature that had started in the 17th century with Descartes was massively accelerated in the 19th century with the exposition, by Darwin[33] and Wallace,[34] of the theory of evolution by natural selection. The fact of evolution itself had long been recognised. Darwin and Wallace proposed a mechanism—an engine—for the generation of natural complexity. It was a mechanism that was to

---

[31]1806–1873.

[32]*On Liberty* (1859).

[33]1809–1882.

[34]1823–1913.

have a profound impact on human self-perception and human thriving. Humans were seen to be part of the natural world. They may be the pinnacle of evolution, but they were produced by the same forces that had produced bacteria, sponges, and dinosaurs. The engine that drove evolution was competition.

This resonated with and reinforced both the Protestant work ethic (a 16th century consequence of seeing humans as distinct, individually responsible units) and with the mechanical view of nature. If nature was de-souled, it could be exploited. And if humans were part of nature, so could they. If humans were part of nature, and nature was shaped by competition (rather than by God), then competition became normative for humans. That is more or less the view of thriving that has pertained since—at least in the west. Its consequences are well documented.

The mechanistic view of humans, together with the identification of competition as the driving force of the human and non-human worlds, had another important consequence. Machines are intrinsically comprehensible and manipulable, and competition rewards effort. This meant, in both popular and academic culture, that human happiness could be planned for and grasped. As we will see, this is simply not the case. As many of the ancients (and notably Aristotle) realised, happiness cannot be approached directly. The more one tries to do so, the more elusive it is. Happiness is a by-product of other activities.

There were, of course, philosophical and political experiments with other models of thriving. Soviet Communists and (more gently) John Rawls,[35] saw the good life in an essentially communitarian way. For Communism, to thrive was to play a vibrant part in the life of the state; for Rawls (who was more concerned about the mechanism for ensuring a just society than with detailed analysis of the elements of that society), thriving entailed ability to shape one's own life, and that in turn required some basic liberties: democratic representation, freedom of association, conscience, and expression, and the right to own personal property (Rawls 1971).

Freud[36] and Jung,[37] though differing very significantly from one another, took seriously the injunction of the Delphic Oracle—'Know thyself', while at the same time agreeing that many or most of the drivers of human action are unconscious and therefore, by definition, immune to examination or ratiocination. For both, to thrive necessitated brokering a peace with the unconscious—whether by active conversation with its ruling (rather Platonic) archetypes (Jung), or by exorcism of the troubling ghosts that stalk the unconscious (Freud).

The post-Second World War existentialists (notably Sartre[38] and Camus,[39] who built on Heidegger's[40] idea of selfhood as a condition of being 'thrown into the world') saw humans as being what they *did*—as self-fashioning. For Sartre this

[35]1921–2002.

[36]1856–1939.

[37]1875–1961.

[38]1905–1980.

[39]1913–1960.

[40]1889–1976.

meant a constant agony of choice: freedom was a burden. To exercise self-fashioning freedom was to fashion others: the weight of doing so was crushing. It is not clear what, if anything, human thriving meant for the Existentialists. The general tone is relentlessly pessimistic. We are urged to be aware of our predicament as wretchedly free beings; and authenticity is praised.

It is hard to generalize about the ruling theories of today—save to say, as we have already done, that autonomy (with its concomitant view of the hard-frontiered individual) is grafted deep into economic and personal presumptions. Many presume that thriving—or at least happiness—can be bought. On one level we are more connected with others than ever before: we are often tethered umbilically, via our computers, with millions of others. Yet it is not clear that this has generated a more communitarian view of ourselves. Ironically our greater connectedness seems to have made us more isolated than ever. That, for animals whose big brains became big precisely because that conferred on us the great selective advantage of being able to be social, is unlikely to be conducive to human thriving. In the next chapter we will see evidence that it is not.

References

Grayling AC (2007) What is good? The search for the best way to live. Phoenix

Kant E (1785) Grounding for the metaphysics of morals, 3rd edn (Transl. Ellington JW) Hackett (1993)

Rawls J (1971) A theory of justice, Harvard University Press

Chapter 3
What Makes Humans Happy?

Abstract Happiness is sometimes thought to be part of living well. This chapter looks at some of the evidence about what makes humans happy. Happiness is surprisingly independent of physical or environmental circumstances: humans are very adaptable. Much of what we are, and much of what contributes to our happiness, is located in our subconscious. Good relationships are important to happiness. So is a sense of significance. Happiness is linked to virtuous behaviour.

Keywords Happiness · Relationality · Virtue · Work · Significance

3.1 Introduction

This is a book about human thriving: about what constitutes the Good Life. There is more to thriving than subjective happiness. Most serious thinkers (at least since Aristotle promulgated his idea of *eudaimonia)* have recognized this. Bentham's 'felicific calculus' is no longer widely approved in the form in which he framed it because (as subsequent utilitarians recognized) there is more to life than feeling good.

But nonetheless subjective happiness matters. And it has the advantage of being easily measured by reference to self-reporting scales. This has resulted in a vast empirical literature. (Stanford 2018, fn 11; Diener and Biswas-Diener 2011).

In this literature there are convoluted debates about terminology and methodology (Stanford Encyclopaedia of Philosophy 2018; Diener et al. 2013; Samman 2007). We concentrate here on 'Psychological' happiness—a category which itself has three main sub-categories: hedonism, life-satisfaction, and emotional state theory. To a first degree of approximation (which is all we need for the present discussion), these three types of approach yield broadly the same conclusions. The work we describe in this chapter results mainly from self-reporting studies. There are obvious objections to such studies, but they remain useful for our large-grained view.

C. Foster and J. Herring, *Human Thriving and the Law*, SpringerBriefs in Law,
https://doi.org/10.1007/978-3-030-01135-2_3

3.2 Conscious and Unconscious Minds and the Conversation Between Them

Philosophers, self-aggrandisingly, like to assume that all they do is a consequence of reason, and they commend this life of reason to others. 'The unexamined life,' opined Socrates, 'is the life not worth living'. But in fact detailed examination of most of our motives seems to be very hard. 'I do not understand what I do', lamented St. Paul. 'For what I want to do I do not do, but what I hate I do. And if I do what I do not want to do, I agree that the law is good. As it is, it is no longer I myself who do it, but it is sin living in me. For I know that good itself does not dwell in me, that is, in my sinful nature. For I have the desire to do what is good, but I cannot carry it out. For I do not do the good I want to do, but the evil I do not want to do—this I keep on doing. Now if I do what I do not want to do, it is no longer I who do it, but it is sin living in me that does it.'[1]

The Buddha agrees: 'My own mind used to wander wherever pleasure or desire or lust let it…' But he claims to have made more progress than St. Paul. 'But now I have it tamed, I guide it, and the keeper guides the wild elephant.'[2]

The American psychologist Jonathan Haidt has adapted the Buddha's metaphor slightly: '*The image that I came up with for myself, as I marvelled at my weakness, was that I was a rider on the back of an elephant. I'm holding the reins in my hands, and by pulling one way or the other I can tell the elephant to turn, to stop, or to go. I can direct things, but only when the elephant doesn't have desires of his own. When the elephant really wants to do something, I'm no match for him*' (Haidt 2006, 4).

In St. Paul, the Buddha, and Jonathan Haidt, we can see the distress—which has a clear and unsurprising emotional component—that comes from being ruled by forces within us but not subject to us. Whatever happiness is, it is compromised by civil war.

It seems improbable that one can broker any peace between the conscious and subconscious factions without having any knowledge of the subconscious faction. But that, of course, presents a big problem. The subconscious is by definition invisible to the eyes of our consciousness.

Yet there are ways of making the usually invisible subconscious more accessible. The obvious example is meditation—in some forms of which the actuating thoughts (usually unnoticed) are specifically examined, and in most forms of which the noise created by the conscious mind is quietened so that the core of the self can be perceived.

The connection between meditation and subjective happiness is well documented: (Choi et al. 2012; Campos et al. 2016; Fredrickson et al. 2008). There may be many levels of explanation for this connection, but one may simply be that there is a

[1]Romans 7: 15–20 (NIV).

[2]*Dhammapada* v 326. Plato uses similar language:

reduction in the internal conflict between the conscious and the unconscious. The Delphic Oracle's injunction 'Know thyself' is likely to make sound psychological sense. But a more general way of expressing what meditation does (and certainly of expressing the particular type of feeling of subjective well-being that results from it) is that it achieves a literal *integrity:* a rather less divided self - or at least a *sense* of a less divided self. Subjective happiness (to state the obvious) is something experienced by a *self.* It is unsurprising that if one has a greater (or less conflicted) sense of what oneself is, the self is likely to be able to experience more pleasure.

A sense of self obviously requires *some* neurological hardware and software. It is not clear that it demands very sophisticated hardware or software. Certainly many non-human species (including the higher apes, cetaceans, and many birds—particularly corvids and parrots) are conscious. No doubt many non-humans beyond the currently recognised classes are conscious too: the better we become at looking for consciousness, the more we find it. We predict that consciousness will ultimately be found to be fairly ubiquitous—as most societies other than our own, very modern one, have presumed that it is.[3]

The elephant and the rider, and other related metaphors, all acknowledge the importance (indeed the overriding importance) of the subconscious in determining our actions, attitudes, and identity. This acknowledgment is contrary to the assumption of most law, most ethics, and much medicine—for which the ability to thrive is inextricably linked to the ability to be cognitive. Thus ethics is often taken to be the business of making reasoned decisions about how to behave —from which it follows that a person not capable of making such decisions (for instance by reason of brain injury) cannot be either ethical or unethical: they are outside the class of persons from whom a moral response is expected. Such a person might have an unconscious disposition to behave in a way that, were it conscious, would be applauded as ethical. That disposition itself might have been created by strenuous moral Aristotelian work when the person was capable of cognition: its presence deep in the subconscious might indicate that the person is particularly deeply moral (as judged by the intransigence of the disposition and the unlikelihood of behaviour contrary to the disposition), but yet, because it is not conscious, it somehow does not count as morality. Identity, similarly, is taken to be evidenced only by actions and words which have had at least some processing by the conscious mind—notwithstanding the fact that much or most of the drivers of those words or actions will be unconscious. Law and ethics, then, in considering who or what is thriving, conclude that the only possible 'thing' that can thrive is the identity produced or evidenced by the (relatively unimportant) conscious mind. That, we suggest, is contrary to the evidence about the contributions of our conscious and our unconscious to the entity that we call our 'self.'

---

[3]For an accessible review of the evidence for animal consciousness, and a cogent criticism of the ways traditionally used to search for it, see Safina, Carl. *Beyond words: What animals think and feel.* Macmillan, 2015.

Conscious attitudes and dispositions are irrationally favoured and the unconscious irrationally ignored or denigrated.

3.3 The Relevance of Bodily Integrity and Physical Environment

Whatever the importance of our unconsciousness, we are embodied creatures. We cannot be certain, of course, but it seems likely that even our unconsciousness is embodied to some degree at least: if our brain dies this might well have some effect on our subconscious. This raises the question of how important bodily integrity and our physical environment are to our happiness.

The starting point is the consensus in the literature that most people describe themselves as happy (Diener and Diener 1996; Biswas-Diener and Diener 2006; Biswas-Diener et al. 2009). '[M]ost environmental and demographic factors', summarizes Jonathan Haidt, '*influence happiness very little*... *White Americans are freed from many of the hassles and indignities that affect black Americans, yet, on average, they are only very slightly happier. Men have more freedom and power than women, yet they are not on average any happier (Women experience more depression, but also more intense joy). The young have so much more to look forward to than the elderly, yet ratings of life satisfaction actually rise slightly with age, up to age sixty-five, and, in some studies, well beyond. People are often surprised to hear that the old are happier than the young because the old have so many more health problems, yet people adapt to most chronic health problems*... *(although ailments that grow progressively worse do reduce well-being, and a recent study finds that adaptation to disability is not, on average, complete). People who live in cold climates expect people who live in California to be happier, but they are wrong. People expect that attractive people are happier than unattractive people, but they, too, are wrong*...' (Haidt 2006, 87–88)

Physical comfort and bodily integrity are, then, not as important to happiness as we might think. And even if they start off being are ranked as important by individuals, that ranking can change very quickly (as Haidt says) when they are lost, increased or diminished: humans quickly accommodate to new conditions. If a set of new circumstances temporarily diminishes happiness, we recalibrate back to, or near to, the happy baseline. Thus, observes Haidt, '[w]ithin a year, lottery winners and paraplegics have both (on average) returned most of the way to their baseline levels of happiness.' (Haidt 2006, 85)

This observation may be a consequence of the physiological habituation of neurone-firing, and/or to the fact, however physiologically mediated, that humans are very sensitive to changes in conditions, but not to absolute levels) (Haidt 2006, 85).[4,5]

3.4 The Significance of Rationality for Human Thriving

We tend to think that our reason is essential to our thriving. This is partly because we assume that the way that we reason is a particularly personal characteristic, and accordingly that 'our' cognition is an essential element of whatever it is that makes us *us* as distinct from any other entity. Thus (we say) the dissolution of the capacity for individual reason entails dissolution of the 'I' which is capable of thriving—*ergo* one cannot thrive without that capacity.

The argument is alluring but shallow. The reasons that we give for conclusions, such as moral positions, are often not reasons at all, but *ex post facto* justifications. The most fundamental parts of us—the parts that really decree what we are, and how we are distinct from others—lie (as Freud and Jung explained) well beneath our consciousness. We will ultimately argue that it follows from this that consciousness is a very overrated characteristic.

We can see many illustrations of this in everyday experience. It is very seldom that *argument* changes minds. Arguments are rarely the causes of our views: they are made up to justify a view that has already been adopted. Haidt demonstrates this compellingly by reference to a story about incest.

Julie and Mark are brother and sister. They are on holiday together. They decide to have sex. Jodie is already on the pill, but just to be absolutely safe , Mark uses a condom. They both enjoy the experience, but resolve never to do it again. It is their secret: it has made them feel closer to each other (Haidt 2006, 20–21).

Haidt examined responses to this story. The overwhelming majority of respondents thought that Julie and Mark's conduct was unacceptable. When asked

---

[4]The fact of accommodation to changed circumstances has an ethically and legally important consequence for advance directives. It has consistently been found that when patients find themselves in the situation anticipated by an advance directive, they are better able to tolerate the new situation than they imagined they would be at the time they made the advance directive: see, e.g., Fagerlin, A. and Schneider, C. E. (2004), 'Enough: The Failure of the Living Will'. Hastings Center Report, 34: 30-42; Fried, T.R., O'leary, J., Van Ness, P. and Fraenkel, L., 2007. 'Inconsistency over time in the preferences of older persons with advanced illness for life-sustaining treatment.' Journal of the American Geriatrics Society, *55*(7), pp. 1007–1014; Sudore R, Fried TR. 'Redefining the 'planning' in advance care planning: preparing for end-of-life decision making.' Ann Intern Med. (2010) Aug 17; 153(4): 256–61.

[5]David Wootton puts the point dramatically: '*A friend of mine, close to death, made a long journey to see the Rothko exhibition at the Tate. He had no doubt there could be no better way to spend what might have been his last day. At such times our choices say a great deal about who we are; much of the rest of the time our answers are not to be trusted.*' 'Desire without end': Times Literary Supplement, 27 February 2009, p. 3.

why, many replied first that incest can result in genetic abnormalities. But when Haidt pointed out that pregnancy would not occur here, what happened?

> …no one says: 'Oh, well, in that case, it's okay.' Instead, people begin searching for other arguments, for example 'It's going to hurt their relationship'. When I respond that in this case the sex has made the relationship stronger, people just scratch their heads, frown, and say: 'I know it's wrong. I'm just having a hard time explaining why.' (Haidt 2006, 21)

> 'If you listen closely to moral arguments', (Haidt summarizes), 'you can sometimes hear something surprising: that it is really the elephant holding the reins, guiding the rider. It is the elephant who decides what is good or bad, beautiful or ugly. Gut feelings, intuitions, and snap judgments happen constantly and automatically….'. (Haidt 2006, 21–22)

The rider does not simply articulate neutrally the policy that has been determined by the elephant: it contends for that policy: '…it becomes a lawyer, fighting in the court of public opinion to persuade others of the elephant's point of view…' (Haidt 2006, 22).

This view is distasteful and unflattering. We preen ourselves as a species on our rationality: on our ability to be ruled not (as we pejoratively say animals are ruled), by appetites, by physiology, by atavistic forces stationed in our subconscious. We like to think that we have dominion over ourselves, and hence over our environments. And the view is doubly distasteful in the Academy, whose ruling presumption (a legacy of the worship of the Classical age)[6] is that arguments convince, and that better arguments convince more.

We look in the next section at some of the unconscious but defining biases that evidence our essentially relational nature. There are other unconscious biases too. A good example is the tendency to see the glass as half empty rather than half full. This makes perfect evolutionary sense: to label an opportunity wrongly as a threat is less dangerous than to label a threat wrongly as an opportunity. The first leads simply to a missed opportunity: the second can lead to you being eaten by a sabre-toothed tiger.[7] We have been designed by Darwin to be Eeyores: to see our glasses as more than half empty. In a marriage, for instance, at least five good or constructive actions are needed to compensate for the damage done by one critical or destructive action (Gottman 1994).

---

[6]Robert Byron put it well: *'The frame upon which the profuse metaphysical speculations of the Roman Mediterranean spluttered to extinction, was the Hellenic subscription to the wholesale efficacy of Reason.... The essence, the fundamental mood of all Greek thought, lay in the problem of the immediae present, in the quest of an ars vivendi...[T]he whole pursuit of 'well-being' was based on a short-sighted rationalism which assumed that once man was aware of his true interests, he must be incapable of action contradictory to them. Hence the grotesque slogan 'Virtue is knowledge'; the implicit belief in the panacea of truth; and the consequent distrust of all instinct and all compromise, the major conditionals of any ars vivendi. This elevation of the mind to supreme control will inevitably find supporters in that class of persons who are more concerned with intellectual processes than the goals to which they lead. But in the majority of human beings, the speculative faculty is either absent or subordinate. Among the masses of the Roman Empire, Greek thought, the kingdom of the mind, had never wholly conquered.' The Byzantine Achievement:* Routledge & Kegan Paul: London and New York (1987): 53–54.

[7]For discussion, see Haidt, ibid, 28–29.

Our brains are plainly connected in some ways to our identity and our essence. But those parts/functions of our brains that govern the conscious, and particularly the consciously reasoning parts of us, seem to be less connected than the parts/functions that contain and mediate the subconscious.[8]

3.5 Sociality and Thriving

In mammals at least, brain size correlates extremely well with the degree of sociability of the species. Correlation is not causation, of course, but we know that relationality demands a large number of neurone-stretching- skills, and it is reasonable to infer causation. Humans have very big brains indeed for their body size, and they are the most social animals we know. If one is looking for the two most obviously definitive human characteristics, big brains and extreme socialization are good candidates.[9] Co-operation and community confer massive selective advantages: it is not surprising that they have been strongly selected for, and that there is a hedonic dividend that makes sociation particularly attractive.

God observed, early in Genesis, that 'it is not good for the man to be alone'.[10] That is a good executive summary of the empirical literature about the importance of sociation. Seneca agreed: 'No one can live happily who has regard to himself alone and transforms everything into a question of his own utility.'[11] And Hinduism and Buddhism are even more radical: happiness demands the ablation of the Self. 'The Way of Heaven is to benefit others', said Lao Tzu.

Although natural selection (while strongly favouring relationality), seems to work primarily at the level of the individual, individual benefits are generally best realized in community—and that entails a conscious or unconscious suppression of the 'I' that will be sociation's eventual beneficiary.

Jonathan Sacks tells a story about a man who wrote to the Lubavitcher Rabbi in something like these terms: 'I feel wretched. I have no pleasures. I have only anxiety. I cannot pray. I cannot see that the situation could ever improve. I am in

---

[8]Iain McGilchrist describes schizophrenia as a 'hypertrophy of reason', in which everything has to be worked out, agonizingly, from first principles, often with bizarre conclusions – partly, at least, because some of the material used for the process of reasoning wells up from the subconscious and is not intended to (and is not, in the normal subject) to be pushed through the machine of conscious reasoning: 'Neuromania: Spiders, yes, but why cats?' Lecture: Oxford University Department for Continuing Education (2014): https://www.youtube.com/watch?v=CkVwGpOXhf8&frags=pl%2Cwn (accessed July 2018).

[9]Along with bipedalism, opposing thumbs, and despite what we have said in the previous section, cognitive firepower.

[10]Genesis 2:18.

[11]Epistle 48, cited Haidt, ibid, 81.

despair. I am desperate for your help.' The Rabbi answered the letter without writing a single word: he merely circled the first word in each sentence.[12]

We have examined elsewhere, in detail, the case for a more explicit acknowledgment by the law of the fact that community, altruism, and relationship are critically connected to general human well-being, (Foster and Herring 2015) and simply observe here that those contentions are buttressed powerfully by the work about the connection between relationality and happiness.

We noted elsewhere, too, that the jobs that give greatest happiness are those that are most helpful to others (Smith 2007), that extroversion (in which people enjoy and benefit from being in the company of others) correlates strongly with happiness, (Shermer 2008), that altruism makes you not only happier (Gittins 2010, 141), but healthier and longer-lived (Brown et al. 2003, 2008, 2009, 2011). Relationality is good, but relationality for the purposes of altruism is even better. Those who self-identify as religious are likely to report being happier (Gittins 2010, 54) and to live longer (or, as Jonathan Sacks says, if you regularly attend religious services perhaps it only *seems* longer). The greater longevity of the religious is probably a consequence of the community affiliation and the associated altruism. Good marriages (in which selflessness is likely to be prominent) are strongly associated with happiness (and not just because naturally happy people are likely to be good at being married—though that may be true). (Waite and Gallagher 2000).[13]

3.6 Work and Significance

Humans are great changers of their environments—for good and for bad. We love objectives, and gain satisfaction when those objectives are achieved. Such satisfaction is greatest when the objective and methods are one's own (Bellah et al. 1985; Kohn and Schooler 1983)[14]—when we are acknowledged as having a significance other than as a cog in a machine. We have seen already that when the work gives a benefit to others, the satisfaction is all the more intense: in such a context it is obvious that we *matter.*

The sense of personal significance and its connection to happiness no doubt account for some of the hedonic effect of relationality and sociation (because it is obvious there that we matter to others, even if there is no formal obligation such as there is between a nurse and a patient) and of religion (because there the believer believes both that they themselves matter to a deity, and that this connotes the sort of moral obligations to others that are known in all contexts to generate feelings of happiness).

[12]Sacks, ibid.

[13]See the discussion in Haidt, ibid, 87–90.

[14]For discussion see Haidt, ibid, 219–226.

3.7 Whatever Happiness Is, Can It Be Pursued?

The literature on relationality suggests that personal happiness is often a by-product: if one seeks personal happiness for its own sake, it will prove elusive, but if one seeks the welfare of others, one will be (incidentally but emphatically) happy. The literature on the link between happiness and work tends in the same direction: if one is engaged passionately in work that one perceives as significant, happiness will be a by-product. The environmental and demographic factors which one can strive to change have, as we have seen, very little effect on happiness. Much of what really controls both our happiness and our motivation lies in our subconscious, and accordingly conscious striving will necessarily be striving towards goals other than the really important ones.

Iain McGilchrist suggests that this is an illustration of a broader and deeper principle: if one seeks to seize anything, there is something in the nature of the act that will cause happiness to drain away. Happiness, therefore, can only be approached indirectly. He locates the reason for this in the (now generally dysfunctional) dialogue between the two cerebral hemispheres. The left hemisphere is an executive: seizing is its business. But it is meant to be an executive acting on the orders of the right hemisphere, which has a more holistic appreciation of the world than the left; which sees the relationships between elements that are perceived by the right as wholly unconnected islands; which is capable of holding together apparently contradictory propositions in a tension that we call wisdom (McGilchrist 2009). Two such propositions might be: 'My happiness is the happiness of another', and 'My happiness is my own'. Happiness is necessarily a holistic entity: one cannot coherently say that one part of me is happy and another is not: it is, therefore, a quality that can only be comprehended by the right hemisphere. If the left seeks to identify and grasp the elements of happiness, it will necessarily miss the target.

3.8 Happiness and Virtue

We saw in Chap. 2 that Aristotle saw human thriving as intimately connected with virtue. A good life, for him, was one that evinced the virtues: a good character was one which tended to cause its bearer to act virtuously. A perfected character was one in which virtue was as natural, effortless, and inevitable as breathing. For most people the context in which the Aristotelian virtuous life is lived will necessarily be vibrantly social—bounded by joyously and/or dutifully shouldered obligation. We saw too that the Judaeo-Christian tradition—at least until Protestantism—agreed. The thriving, virtuous man is no solitary. He is embedded in a community, and does not distinguish between its interests and his own. Like the Aristotelian virtuous man, he sprouts virtue: he is 'like a tree planted by streams of water, that yields its fruit in its season, and its leaf does not wither. In all that he does, he prospers.'[15] This, the Psalmist makes clear, comes with a particularly robust type of happiness.

This is a picture that accords well with the empirical literature about happiness. It feels good to be good.

But what does it mean to be good?

Martin Seligman, best known for the 'positive psychology' movement, along with his co-worker Chris Paterson, scoured the literature of many cultures to see what, if anything, was universally regarded as virtuous. They found that there was substantial agreement. This is what advocates of natural law had always said was the case. Here, for instance, is C.S.Lewis:

> The Tao, which others may call Natural Law or Traditional Morality or the First Principles of Practical Reason or the First Platitudes, is not one among a series of possible systems of value. It is the sole source of all value judgments. If it is rejected, all value is rejected. If any value is retained, it is retained. The effort to refute it and raise a new system of value in its place is self-contradictory. There has never been, and never will be, a radically new judgment of value in the history of the world. What purport to be new systems or... ideologies...all consist of fragments from the Tao itself, arbitrarily wrenched from their context in the whole and then swollen to madness in their isolation, yet still owing to the Tao and to it alone such validity as they possess. (Lewis 1943)

Paterson and Seligman found that six broad categories of virtue were ubiquitous: Wisdom, courage, humanity, justice, temperance, and transcendence (by which they meant the capacity to connect to something outside and greater than oneself).

What character traits facilitate the establishment and flourishing of these virtues? Peterson and Seligman identified twenty four traits (Peterson and Seligman 2004)[16]:

Wisdom-facilitating traits:

- curiosity
- love of learning
- judgment
- ingenuity
- emotional intelligence
- perspective

Courage-facilitating traits:

- valour
- perseverance
- integrity

Humanity-facilitating traits

- kindness
- loving

---

[15]Psalm 1:3. There is a very similar description in Jeremiah 17:8.

[16]See the discussion in Haidt, ibid, 167–170.

Justice-facilitating traits

- citizenship
- fairness
- leadership

Temperance-facilitating traits

- self-control
- prudence
- humility

Transcendence-facilitating traits

- appreciation of beauty and excellence
- gratitude
- hope
- spirituality
- forgiveness
- humour
- zest

We note that most of these traits do not require either sophisticated higher cortical function or a high degree of bodily integrity. Indeed many of them may be frustrated by very efficient cognition, or enhanced by physical or mental compromise. If virtue is connected to happiness, then, it does not begin to follow that happiness is a function of a sound body or an efficient brain. And if thriving is defined more broadly than in terms of happiness (if, for instance, a criterion of 'satisfaction' or 'significance' is added to the definition), the connection with bodily or mentally function becomes even more tenuous.

3.9 Conclusion

There is a vast and contentious scientific literature on what in fact makes humans happy. There are important and highly technical disputes about what 'happiness' is, and how to measure it. But some conclusions emerge clearly. They are not counterintuitive, but they are rather counter-cultural—at least in the modern west.

Environmental and demographic factors (including physical ability) affect happiness very little. Humans have a great capacity to adapt fast to changing circumstances, and circumstances that seemed unbearable in prospect become perfectly compatible with happiness when they eventuate. Happiness entails good relationships, good relationships entail a shift of focus from oneself to another, and the extreme manifestation of that shift, altruism, is particularly closely associated with happiness both in work and outside work. A feeling of significance makes us feel happy: that significance comes particularly from relationships and from work that does good to others.

Being virtuous—in the sense of behaving in a way concordant with one of the universally acknowledged—also encourages happiness: perhaps by facilitating relationality: perhaps because many virtues are outward-looking and tend towards altruism.

Many types of happiness, and many of the qualities associated with happiness, are unconnected with cognitive or physical integrity. Much happiness seems to bubble up from beneath consciousness, and humans adapt fast and thoroughly to even dramatic changes in circumstances or physical ability.

Whatever happiness is, it will slip out of your fingers if you try to grasp it directly. It is only ever a by-product.

References

Bellah R, Madsen R, Sullivan WM, Swidler A, Tipton S (1985) Habits of the heart. Harper and Row, New York

Biswas-Diener R, Diener ED (2006) The subjective well-being of the homeless, and lessons for happiness. Soc Indic Res 76(2):185–205

Biswas-Diener R., Vittersø J., Diener E. (2009) Most people are pretty happy, but there is cultural variation: the Inughuit, the Amish, and the Maasai. In: Diener E. (eds) Culture and Well-Being. Social Indicators Research Series, vol 38. Springer, Dordrecht

Brown S, Nesse R, Vinokur AD, Smith DM (2003) Providing support may be more beneficial than receiving it: results from a prospective study of mortality. Psychol Sci 14:320–327

Brown SL, Brown RM, House JS, Smith DM (2008) Coping with spousal loss: the potential buffering effects of self-reported helping behavior. Personal Soc Psychol Bull 34:849–861

Brown SL, Smith DM, Schulz R, Kabeto M, Ubel P, Yee J, Langa K (2009) Caregiving and decreased mortality in a national sample of older adults. Psychol Sci 20:488–494

Brown SL, Brown RM, Preston S (2011) A model of human caregiving motivation. In: Brown S, Brown R, Penner S (eds) Moving beyond self interest: perspectives from evolutionary biology, neuroscience, and the social sciences. Oxford University Press, New York

Campos D, Cebolla A, Quero S, Bretón-López J, Botella C, Soler J, García-Campayo J, Demarzo M, Baños RM (2016) Meditation and happiness: Mindfulness and self-compassion may mediate the meditation–happiness relationship. Personality Individ Differ 93:80–85

Choi Y, Karremans JC, Barendregt H (2012) The happy face of mindfulness: Mindfulness meditation is associated with perceptions of happiness as rated by outside observers. J Positive Psychol 7(1):30–35

Diener E, Diener C (1996) Most people are happy. Psychol Sci 7(3):181–185

Diener E, Biswas-Diener, R (2011) Happiness: unlocking the mysteries of psychological wealth. Wiley

Diener E, Inglehart R, Tay L (2013) Theory and validity of life satisfaction scales. Soc Indic Res 112(3):497–527

Foster C, Herring J (2015) Altruism. Welfare and the Law, Springer, London

Fredrickson BL, Cohn MA, Coffey KA, Pek J, Finkel SM (2008) Open hearts build lives: positive emotions, induced through loving-kindness meditation, build consequential personal resources. J Pers Soc Psychol 95(5):1045

Gittins R (2010) The happy economist: happiness for the hard-headed. Allen & Unwin, CrowsNest, NSW

Gottman J (1994) Why marriages succeed or fail. Simon and Schuster, New York

Haidt J (2006) The happiness hypothesis: putting ancient wisdom and philosophy to the test of modern science, Arrow

Kohn ML, Schooler C (1983) Work and personality: An inquiry into the impact of social stratification. Ablex, Norwood, NJ

Lewis CS (1943) The abolition of man. OUP, Oxford

McGilchrist I (2009) The master and his emissary: the divided brain and the making of the western World. Yale University Press, Newhaven

Peterson C, Seligman MEP (2004) Character strengths and virtues: a handbook and classification. American Psychological Association and OUP, Washington DC

Samman E (2007) Psychological and subjective well-being: a proposal for internationally comparable indicators. Oxf Dev Stud 35(4):459–486

Shermer M (2008) The mind of the market: compassionate apes, competitive humans, and other tales from evolutionary economics. Macmillan, London

Smith T (2007) Job satisfaction in the United States: America's general social survey. National Opinion Research Centre, University of Chicago, Chicago

Stanford Encyclopedia of Philosophy, Happiness' https://plato.stanford.edu/entries/happiness/#EmpFin. Accessed July 2018

Waite LJ, Gallagher M (2000) The case for marriage: why married people are happier, healthier, and better off financially. Doubleday, New York

Chapter 4
Thriving, Care and Vulnerability

Abstract This chapter explores the role of care and vulnerability in a thriving life. It argues that humans are by nature vulnerable beings. This nature entails many good things. It requires us to reach out to others to find co-operative solutions to the issues we face; it requires us to change and be open to new ideas and ways of thinking as we relate to other people; it ensures that relationships are at the heart of our lives; it means we do not need to (and should not) pretend that we are autonomous rational beings; and it means that care is essential to our survival and the source of much that is good about life. A thriving human life is, therefore, one marked by care and vulnerability.

Keywords Autonomy · Care · Disability · Openness · Relationality
Vulnerability

4.1 Introduction

In this chapter we argue that vulnerability and care are central to the concept of human thriving. It is striking how the opposite is often claimed in the media and by politicians.

Being vulnerable is seen as a stigmatic term, and hence in the Care Act 2014 the language of 'vulnerable adult' was replaced with talk of adults 'in need of services'. Being in a vulnerable group is said to justify paternalistic intervention, with the aim of restoring the vulnerable person to a position that lacks vulnerability. Margrit Shildrick (2002, 71) noted that, 'in western modernity at least, vulnerability is figured as a shortcoming, an impending failure'. Being vulnerable is a source of shame, a state to be overcome. We claim the opposite. It is the core of a thriving life.

Care is seen as a 'problem' and a source of disadvantage. A good example of this is that children who care for their disabled relatives are seen as suffering a terrible disadvantage. The Daily Mirror refers to: 'Brave youngsters who are losing out on their childhood as they are caring for their sick mums' (Beck 2014). The Daily Mail claims that young carers have 'no time for childhood', and explains that: 'Looking after a disabled relative is exhausting and stressful. It's bad enough for the adults

C. Foster and J. Herring, *Human Thriving and the Law*, SpringerBriefs in Law,
https://doi.org/10.1007/978-3-030-01135-2_4

who have to do it, but what's it like for the estimated 175,000 British children whose lives are spent caring for a parent or sibling?' (Moorhead 2009) David Mowat, the former Minister for Community Health and Care claimed in the introduction to a report on Young Carers (*Ambition Interrupted*: HM Government 2017) that when children have to take on care work 'hopes and dreams can be derailed'.

We argue in this chapter that such approaches are seriously misguided and that care and vulnerability are essential features of a thriving life. The image of the person promoted and assumed by the law (an autonomous, self-sufficient, capable person) is, if it is possible at all, a wretched state to be in. We need to rejoice in our vulnerability and in our care.

4.2 Vulnerability and Thriving

Vulnerability has its origin in the Latin word 'vulnerare' meaning 'to wound'. Doris Schroeder and Eugenijus Gefenas (2009) distinguish between the external element of vulnerability (being exposed to the possibility of harm) and the internal element (being substantially unable to protect oneself from the possibility of harm). They, therefore, define vulnerability in this way:

> To be vulnerable means to face a significant probability of incurring an identifiable harm while substantially lacking ability and/or means to protect oneself.

We suggest that a person (P) is vulnerable if the following three factors are present:

1. P faces a risk of harm.
2. P does not have the resources to be able to avoid the risk of harm materializing
3. P would not be able to respond adequately to the harm if the risk materialized. (see Herring 2016, ch 1 for further discussion).

To clarify our understanding of vulnerability we distinguish two ways in which vulnerability is used in the literature. The first we call 'particular deficient vulnerability'—vulnerability seen as an undesirable condition suffered by particular individuals or groups of people. This a condition that we should seek to eliminate or alleviate as much as possible. The second we call 'universal beneficial vulnerability': vulnerability seen as a desirable attribute of all humankind, which we should embrace (Fienman 2008; Herring 2016, 2018). This is a view associated particularly with the writing of Fineman (2008, 1). She argues that:

> The vulnerability approach recognizes that individuals are anchored at each end of their lives by dependency and the absence of capacity. Of course, between these ends, loss of capacity and dependence may also occur, temporarily for many and permanently for some as a result of disability or illness. Constant and variable throughout life, individual vulnerability encompasses not only damage that has been done in the past and speculative harms of the distant future, but also the possibility of immediate harm. We are beings who

> live with the ever-present possibility that our needs and circumstances will change. On an individual level, the concept of vulnerability (unlike that of liberal autonomy) captures this present potential for each of us to become dependent based upon our persistent susceptibility to misfortune and catastrophe.

We support this second view, and have argued for it elsewhere (Foster and Herring 2017; Herring 2016, 2018). We will not repeat those reasons here, but will instead explore further why it is that we should not only accept that vulnerability is at the heart of humanity, but should rejoice that this is so.

4.3 Mutuality and Vulnerability

Because we are all at risk and facing a range of harms that we cannot on our own protect ourselves against, we have to join with others. We have to offer and receive help from others to respond to our mutual vulnerabilities. This requires us to be open to our own needs and those of others. An acknowledgement of human vulnerability promotes empathy and compassion (Feder Kittay 2011). It helps generate intimacy and trust. It compels us to focus on interactive, co-operative solutions to the issues we address. It requires creativity to find how our different skills, limitations and characters can be combined to find effective responses to the risks we face. As Carse (2006, 48) puts it: '*Our vulnerability is inextricably tied to our capacity to give of ourselves to others, to treasure and aspire, to commit to endeavours, to care about justice and about our own and other's dignity.*'

This call to co-operation and mutual understanding is central to our human thriving and results in some of the greatest of human achievements. Consider, for instance, the sculpture of Gustav Vigeland, the painting of Gwen Jones, the buildings of Winay Wayna, and Serena Williams in full flow. These are all the result of the efforts of many people combining their strengths and weaknesses to produce together something that no one of them, in their vulnerable state, could have produced alone.

Yet our society tends to overlook this. The managing director receives an enormous bonus to reflect the work of all who work 'under' him. The Government minister takes the credit for the successful implementation of a policy. We make much of the special provisions given to enable disabled people to have access (Fine and Glendinning 2005), pretending there are no provisions that enable the so-called able bodied to have access. Success for a person with a disability is measured by the extent to which they may be able to be (or present themselves as being) independent and autonomous (Shakespeare 2000). Yet *none* of us can reach that state without considerable support from society and those around us (Fineman 2012). So, our mutual vulnerability encourages us—indeed requires us—to reach out to others, to join forces, to recognise our different strengths and weaknesses, our limitations and gifts, and so to produce far greater things than we can on our own. Vulnerability facilitates co-operation, which is, as any evolutionary biologist knows, a very potent force.

4.4 Openness and Vulnerability

The inevitable vulnerability of our selves mean that we have to be open to change. We must respond to the risks we face and be ready to interact with others to find solutions to the vulnerabilities we face together. As Gilson (2013) argues, vulnerability is an 'open-ended condition that makes possible learning, love, affection, and self-transformation just as much as it makes possible suffering and harm'. If we were simply in control of our lives and perfectly and consistently autonomous, we would continue to plough the same furrow. But because we have to respond to and work with those with whom we are in relationship, we have to be open to change. As Nussbaum (2001) has argued, such relational goods require 'openness towards the world and its possibilities… a yielding and receptive character of soul that is not compatible with an undue emphasis on self-protection.'

We must realise too that bodies change during the course of our lives. This itself opens up new possibilities of interaction with the world. Many non-human organisms play a central role to the maintenance of our bodies. We are less us than we like to think! (Chau and Herring 2014). We are dependent on others for survival, and subject to environmental factors. Our true sense of self and identity is not found in our bounded, owned body, but in the breaking, mixing, and interaction of our bodies with others and with the wider environment (Chau and Herring 2014). As Kenneth Gergen (2009, 23) writes:

> [T]he idea of the skin as a container seems inappropriate. The metaphor of a sieve might be more relevant, with material moving in both directions. On the one hand we could say that nothing that passes through me is distinctly mine (my body); all that I call 'my body' belongs to the larger world out of which it is but a transient conglomerate.

The contrast between the firm youthful body and the wrinkled older body is a false contrast. The frail, previous, mutable, fragile, interdependent body presented as an older body is in fact the truth for *all* bodies. This is a more exciting, dynamic and accurate understanding of 'body' than the biologically and sociologically false claims that the mythical 'youthful body' is static, constrained and independent.

All of these aspects of vulnerability require us to have an openness to the unbidden (Sandel 2004). They stop us getting 'into a rut' and help us thrive.

4.5 Relationships and Vulnerability

If we wanted to try to avoid vulnerability, we would avoid entering relationships. Relationships rely on trust and being open with another. But these create risks that one's trust will be exploited or one's openness exploited. As Jo Bridgeman (2006) puts it 'Humans are vulnerable…because we care, love, are intimately connected to others.'

These risks are an inevitable part of relationships, but relationships are central to human well being. Sevenhuijsen (1998) puts it like this:

> We are in danger of not meeting our obligations; we are risk of others not meeting theirs to us. Relationship can be used as a tool of abuse and in relationships we are open to being abused.

However, at the same time these relationships give us the seeds we need for thriving. Phillips (2011, 139) rightly says:

> Helplessness is the precondition for human bonds, for exchange; you have to be a helpless subject in order to be helped, in order to be understood, in order to become a moral creature. And so, by the same token, if you can't experience helplessness you are precluded from these fundamental human experiences.

Relationships are inextricably tied to our identity. It is through our relationships with others that our selves emerge. Butler (2004, 22) notes that:

> It is not as if an 'I' exists independently over here and then simply loses a 'you' over there, especially if the attachment to 'you' is part of what composes who 'I' am. If I lose you, under these conditions, then I not only mourn the loss, but I become inscrutable to myself. Who 'am' I, without you? When we lose some of these ties by which we are constituted, we do not know who we are or what to do. On one level, I think that I have lost 'you' only to discover that 'I' have gone missing as well. At another level, perhaps what I have lost 'in' you, that for which I have no ready vocabulary, is a relationality that is composed neither exclusively of myself nor you, but is to be conceived as the tie by which those terms are differentiated and related.

If relationship with others is what produces identity, then identity itself is inherently vulnerable—but not in a bad way (Drichel 2013). To quote Butler again:

> One does not always stay intact. One may want to, or manage to for a while, but despite one's best efforts, one is undone, in the face of the other, by the touch, by the scent, by the feel, by the prospect of the touch, by the memory of the feel (Butler 2004).

4.6 Personhood and Vulnerability

In, *Identity, Personhood and the Law* (Foster and Herring 2017) we made the case for relational personhood. We argued there that personhood (understood as the category of being which has the highest moral claim) emerges from relationships of care.

We rejected the view of some commentators that it is our rationality, or our intellectual capabilities, or our species membership which generate personhood. We argued that value, dignity and humanity do not consist in or proceed from our intellect, but consist in and proceed from our feelings, our relationships, our care, and our love. It is because we are vulnerable that we come to value not our separate personal capacities but the relations between us. And love is therefore at the heart of human thriving. Neal (2012) puts it well:

> We are beings who strive for—and achieve—the sublime, the awe-inspiring, and the transcendent. We aspire to be, not just animals, but moral beings: to pursue second order preferences and desires; to hold ourselves and others to standards of behaviour that surpass

> those we tolerate from other animals and would settle for from ourselves if we were content to fulfil only the animal side of our nature; and we characteristically hope for immortality, either in the literal sense of "life after death", or in a secular sense through the legacies of our work (art, invention, discovery) and the personal marks we leave on those whose lives have intersected with our own (we wish not to be forgotten).

It is important to note that it is the relationships emerging from our vulnerable nature which generate the highest moral status, rather than our intellect or our autonomy. This shows that young and old, able-minded and those of limited intellectual ability, the disabled and the abled-bodied are all equally valuable, because our vulnerabilities require us to be in relationships. It is that most human of characteristics—caring relationships which are created by our vulnerable selves—that generates our moral value and is the cornerstone of our thriving.

4.7 Autonomy and Vulnerability

Autonomy is closely linked to being invulnerable. And since invulnerability is an illusion, so too is autonomy. Yet as Diduck (2013) argues, both the literature and the *zeitgeist* suggest strongly that 'autonomy is to be respected and promoted while vulnerability is to be pitied, remedied or alleviated'. Indeed in legal thinking autonomy has come to play a central role, as a cornerstone of our understanding of our right to be able to make our own choices about how to act, and our right to be subject only to those responsibilities we choose to assume. These rights are seen as the central pillars of the economic, social and legal structures (Herring 2016). Yet this is rests on the highly dubious assumption that we are masters of our own destinies.

We deceive ourselves into thinking we have capacity to make decisions. Our decision-making processes are flawed. We take into account falsehoods; we are unduly influenced by others; we act in irrational ways. We do not move through life pursuing a rationally devised life-plan that has taken into account all the relevant information and all the possible contingencies. We are all muddled, irrational, irascible, emotionally driven, incoherent thinkers and deciders (Herring 2016). We are not, thank goodness, slaves of our minds or rational thought or logic. We are creatures of blood, love, wildness and eccentricity.

Jesse Wall has argued that to act autonomously it must be shown that a person is able:

- to act free from undue interference or influence of others (the freedom condition)
- to exercise the capacity for rational thought and cognition (the competence condition) and
- to act according to the beliefs, values, and commitments that the person identifies or endorses as their own beliefs, values, and commitments (the authenticity condition) (Wall 2017).

Mackenzie and Rogers (2013) argue, to similar effect, that to be able to exercise autonomy, we need to display the following characteristics:

- ***Self-determination*** This refers to the ability:

  > . . . to determine one's own beliefs, values, goals and wants, and to make choices regarding matters of practical import to one's life free from undue interference. The obverse of self-determination is determination by other persons, or by external forces or constraints.

- ***Self-government*** This refers to the ability:

  > . . . to make choices and enact decisions that express, or are consistent with, one's values, beliefs and commitments. Whereas the threats to self-determination are typically external, the threats to self-governance are typically internal, and often involve volitional or cognitive failings. Weakness of will and failures of self-control are common volitional failings that interfere with self-governance.

- ***Having authenticity***

  > [A] person's decisions, values, beliefs and commitments must be her 'own' in some relevant sense; that is, she must identify herself with them and they must cohere with her 'practical identity', her sense of who she is and what matters to her. Actions or decisions that a person feels were foisted on her, which do not cohere with her sense of herself, or from which she feels alienated, are not autonomous.

Their point is that if these conditions are not fulfilled then a person cannot really be taken to have chosen a course of action for themselves. Others have imposed values upon them, or they are not able to use their values to make decisions for themselves. Imagine a woman who is in a relationship of domestic abuse. She has reached a position where she simply obeys her partner on every issue. In such a case, respecting her decisions is not respecting her autonomy. One might question how often anyone meets all of the conditions demanded by Wall or McKenzie and Rogers.

The inevitable concern about a claim that questions our capacity to make decisions is that it will lead to corrosive paternalism. But it does not. If we are all flawed, vulnerable decision makers that is as true for doctors, judges and social workers as it is for everyone else. Indeed the universal beneficial vulnerability theory seems to be the most powerful critique of paternalism available. It does not assume that autonomy is the only basis of respect for someone's decisions: there are other good reasons for such respect (Herring 2016). If we start, as the universal beneficial vulnerability model does, by assuming that people are vulnerable, interdependent, and caring, the nature of legal intervention becomes different. Upholding and maintaining those relationships becomes a central objective of the law. A law based on this assumption would not emphasise independence, liberty, or autonomy, but would instead seeks to buttress relationships and promote care (Foster and Herring 2015)

Indeed, a refusal to recognise our mutual vulnerability creates paternalism. It encourages those who regard themselves as competent as being thereby authorised to control the incompetent. One of us (Herring 2018) has used the example of childhood to show that, because parents imagine children to be vulnaerble, (while parents are rational and capacitiious), parents are authorised to control children.

We argue that once parents realise that they are as vulnerable as children, the hierarchical model of parenting can be set aside. Failure to recognise one's own vulnerability results in a failure of care which is itself a cause of (potentially toxic) vulnerability in the other.

Eva Feder Kittay, a widely respected American academic has a daughter, Sesha, who has cerebral palsy. Sesha is profoundly cognitively and physically impaired. She will always be dependent on others for life's basics. Feder Kittay (2011, 621) writes:

> Sometimes I wonder if Sesha is a special being sent to us from elsewhere, for there is an impossible to - articulate sweetness, graciousness, and emotional openness about her—qualities we rarely find in others. On any conventional definition of health, Sesha would be found unhealthy, but does not her sweetness, graciousness and openness demonstrate a rare health. We elevate the capacity for logic, rational thought and autonomy over the capacity for wonder, gentleness and warmth, but perhaps the first set of qualities make for a better person than the other.

Kittay concludes her discussion of dignity with a central point: '*I urge that we not look for the basis of dignity in attributions we have as individuals, but in the relationships we bear to one another.*' We likewise suggest that the source of value, dignity, and humanity is not our intellect but our feelings, relationships, care, and love: these all flow from our mutual vulnerability (see further Foster and Herring 2017).

When we recognise our own vulnerability, and hence our lack of capacity or autonomy, we are freed from the shackles of autonomy. We don't have to pretend that we are rational and thoughtful. We don't need to go to enormous lengths to ensure that we are fully informed about every conceivably relevant fact. We should focus on promoting caring relationships and acting in love. We do not have to ape computers. We can be human.

4.8 Vulnerability and Compassion

Compassion has many links with vulnerability. As argued above, if we acknowledge our mutual vulnerability, we will reach out to others. Because vulnerability is *mutual,* the consequent compassion will not be paternalistic. Instead of one person exercising compassion over another, we should be compassionate with one another.

4.9 Care

The other core aspect of thriving is care. One of us has written a whole book on the value of caring relationships (Herring 2013) and so we will be brief. It follows from what has been said about our vulnerable nature that caring for others by meeting their needs is an inevitable part of being human (Fineman 2004, p. xvii). Throughout our lives we should be, and generally are, in caring relationships. They are enormously valuable. Robin West (2002, 89) puts it like this:

> Caregiving labor (and its fruits) is the central adventure of a lifetime; it is what gives life its point, provides it with meaning, and returns to those who give it some measure of security and emotional sustenance. For even more of us, whether or not we like it and regardless of how we regard it, caregiving labor, for children and the aged, is the work we will do that creates the relationships, families, and communities within which our lives are made pleasurable and connected to something larger than ourselves.

We need a legal and social response that recognises that caring is an activity of central importance. If we are relational, vulnerable and interconnected, it is clear that care is essential to human thriving. Our legal system should put the sustenance of caring relationships at its heart (Herring 2013).

We must recognise that we all need social provision and support for survival. These are not required only by the people we designate as 'vulnerable' or 'failing'. The important matter is not who gets these benefits (in a civilized society we all do) but how they are distributed.

Our interactions with each other should be governed by a responsibility to ensure that we do not exploit each other's vulnerability. For example, one of us has promoted a contract law along the following lines:

> Where all contracting parties are encouraged to recognize each other's vulnerability and act in good faith towards each other, providing them with the information they need, doing what they can to ensure the other is not mistaken or entering a clearly unfair bargain. Where the values promoted are honesty, mutuality and interdependence (Herring 2016, ch 6).

This is very different from our current contract law which seems designed to enable exploitation of the weak party, squeeze as a high price as possible, and ensure that neither contracting party will ever want to speak to the other again!

A recognition of our mutual vulnerability delights in the fact that we cannot be self-sufficient, self-contained, autonomous individuals. By our very nature our well-being is dependent on relationships and mutuality. The structures of our law and social interventions need to move away from protecting individual rights and towards promoting caring relationships and flourishing communities.

Of course the law can play only a small part in promoting and protecting a care-valuing ethos. But the law can send important messages about the standards of behaviour expected. Legal regulations and the messages from them force or nudge people in various ways. They provide generalised guidance as to how people arrange their interactions. Court cases are but a small part of how the law operates. The law can be involved in creating an environment in which compassionate caring relationships flourish—just as contract law plays a role in creating an environment in which contracts are respected. Through the provision of state support and financial protections, we can design our state support mechanisms in a way that follows an ethic of care. We are beginning to see support through welfare payments for those who undertake the care of others, although this is limited. Employment law offers protection to those who undertake paid work and have caring responsibilities. One of us has discussed elsewhere the broad range of areas in which this might make the task of compassionate caring relationships easier and less a source of social disadvantage (Herring 2013).

4.10 Conclusion

Susan Dodds argues that we need a legal and social system which is premised not on individualistic conceptions of autonomy but an acceptance of our vulnerability:

> A vulnerability-centered view of the self and of persons is better able to capture many of our moral motivations and intuitions than can be captured by an autonomy-focused approach. We are all vulnerable to the exigencies of our embodied, social and relational existence and, in recognizing this inherent human vulnerability, we can see the ways in which a range of social institutions and structures protect us against some vulnerabilities, while others expose us to risk. We do not have to view our obligations towards those who lack the capacity to develop or retain autonomy as having a different source from our obligations towards those whose autonomy is made vulnerable due to a degree of dependency. It may be easier to recognize the social value of provision of care if it is viewed as something on which we all have been dependent and on which we are all likely to be dependent at different points in our lives, rather than altruistic behaviour extended to those who lack 'full personhood.' (Dodds 2007)

We have argued that such an approach would help promote human thriving. It would shift legal interventions away from the promotion of self-sufficiency, individualised conceptions of rights and the elevation of autonomy as a central value. Instead it would promote human flourishing by recognising our mutual vulnerability and by putting the promotion of caring relationships at the heart of legal responses.

References

Beck S (2014) 'Brave youngsters who are losing out on their childhood as they are caring for their sick mums' The Daily Mirror, 11 November 2014

Bridgeman J (2006) Book review. Feminist Legal Stud 14:407–410

Butler J (2004) Precarious life. Verso, London

Carse A (2006) Vulnerability, agency and human flourishing. In: Taylor C, Dell'Oro R (eds) Health and Human Flourishing. Georgetown University Press, Washington

Chau P-L, Herring J (2014) Interconnected, inhabited and insecure: why bodies should not be property. J Med Ethics 44:39–45

Diduck A (2013) Autonomy and vulnerability in family law: The missing link. In: J. Wallbank, J. Herring (eds) Vulnerabilities, care and family law. Routledge, Abingdon

Dodds S (2007) Depending on care: recognition of vulnerability and the social contribution of care provision. Bioethics 21:500

Drichel S (2013) Reframing vulnerability: 'So Obviously the Problem. ? SubStance 42:3–25

Feder Kittay E (2011) Forever small: the strange case of Ashley X. Hypatia 26:610–642

Fine M, Glendinning C (2005) Dependence, independence or interdependence? Revisiting the concepts of 'care' and 'dependency. Ageing Soc 21:601–631

Fineman M (2004) The autonomy myth. New Press, New York

Fineman M (2008) The vulnerable subject: anchoring equality in the human condition Yale J Law Feminism 20:1–93

Fineman M (2012) 'Elderly' as vulnerable: Rethinking the nature of individual and societal responsibility. Elder Law J 20:71–145

Foster C, Herring J (2015) Altruism, Welfare and the Law. Springer, London

Foster C, Herring J (2017) Identity, Personhood and the Law. Springer, London
Gergen K (2009) Relational Being. Oxford University Press, Oxford
Gilson E (2013) The ethics of vulnerability: a feminist analysis of social life and practice. Routledge, New York
Herring J (2013) Caring and the law. Hart, Oxford
Herring J (2016) Vulnerable adults and the law. OUP, Oxford
Herring J (2018) Childhood, vulnerability and the law. Springer, Berlin
Neal M (2012) 'Not Gods but animals': Human dignity and vulnerable subjecthood. Liverpool Law Rev 33:177–198
HM Government (2017) Ambition interrupted. The Stationary Office, London
Mackenzie C, Rogers W (2013) Autonomy, vulnerability and capacity: a philosophical appraisal of the Mental Capacity Act. Int J Law Context 9:37–52
Moorhead J (2009) 'No time for childhood.' Daily Mail 28 Febuary 2009
Nussbaum M (2001) The fragility of goodness: luck and ethics in Greek tragedy and philosophy. Cambridge University Press, Cambridge
Phillips A (2011) Freud's helplessness. In: Levine G (ed) The joy of secularism. Princeton University Press, Princeton NJ
Sandel M (2004) The case against perfection. The Atlantic, April 2004
Schroder D, Gefenas E (2009) Vulnerability: too vague and too broad. Cambridge Quarterly Healthcare Ethics 18:113–131
Sevenhuijsen S (1998) Citizenship and the ethics of care. Routledge, London
Shakespeare T (2000) Help. Verso, London
Shildrick M (2002) Embodying the monster: encounters with the vulnerable self. Routledge, London
Wall J (2017) Being yourself: Authentic decision-making and depression. In: Foster C, Herring J (eds) Depression: law and ethics. Oxford University Press, Oxford, pp 134–144
West R (2002) The Right to Care. In: Feder Kittay E (ed) The subject of care: feminist perspectives on dependency. Rowman & Littlefield, Lanham, pp 89–103

Chapter 5
Making It Work: Ideas of Human Thriving in Practice

Abstract This chapter seeks to apply the principles of human thriving articulated in the book to seven situations: cosmetic surgery in an effort to make a human look like a wolf; coerced breast augmentation; PVS; personality change in dementia; the extraction of sperm from a man with brain injury; a dispute about how children should be educated; and assisted suicide.

Keywords Cosmetic surgery · Coercion · PVS · Dementia · Suicide

5.1 Introduction

In this book we have surveyed and criticized the ways in which the notion of human thriving has been understood since the time that humans first emerged. We have noted that vulnerability, mutability, and the shouldering and donation of the 'burden' of care are part of the normal human condition. We have never met the autonomous person whom much of law and ethics assume is the normal or at least the desirable person, and if such a person does exist, we would, on the evidence, expect them to be miserable, and miserably bad company. Humans are amongst the most social of animals, and, however human thriving is described, (whether by reference to happiness or otherwise) humans thrive best in communities—membership of which entails obligation. If happiness is connected to thriving, it is important to note that happiness is remarkably independent of many physical and environmental conditions: humans very quickly accommodate to changes, both positive and negative, that we tend to assume would have a massive positive or negative effect on our happiness. We have noted that thriving has often been understood as involving virtuous behaviour—and that acting virtuously often *feels* good. There is very substantial agreement across cultures about what the core virtues are, and many of the virtues, as well as many of the central pleasures, are not dependent on good cognitive function. We have observed that much human motivation—and much, more generally, much of what makes human X distinct from human Y, wells up from the sub-conscious. Accordingly we consider that

C. Foster and J. Herring, *Human Thriving and the Law*, SpringerBriefs in Law,
https://doi.org/10.1007/978-3-030-01135-2_5

cognition, and indeed consciousness (the nature and footprints of which are mysterious), are given inappropriate weight in determinations both of questions of identity and of the best interests of individuals.

We began the book by looking at the way that the law approaches determinations of the 'best interests' of incapacitous adults and children. We saw that the law often assumes that to thrive is to be autonomous, and we were critical of that assumption.

Having criticized the way that the English law views the Good Life—and hence how it makes 'best interests' determinations, it is only fair that we say how we think the determinations should be done, and in particular what account of human thriving should be embodied in such determinations.

In this chapter we discuss a number of scenarios which turn on the issue of human thriving. We (the two authors) supply separate answers to these questions. Sometimes we agree: sometimes we do not. We make no apology for the divergence: quite the opposite.

5.2 Scenario 1: Becoming a Wolf

Ian is besotted with wolves. He spends as much time with them as he can, and feels closer to them than he does to humans. He visits his local private plastic surgeon (Sarah) and asks her to undertake a procedure that will make him look as much like a wolf as possible. Sarah is willing to perform the necessary complex procedures, involving skin grafts and implants, on payment of a substantial fee. Ian pays and in due course become lupine.

5.2.1 The Law

Following the decisions in *R v Brown*[1] and *R v BM*[2] (see Ch 1) the law is relatively straightforward. Any procedure involving actual bodily harm or a more serious injury, (as Ian's surgery certainly will) will, prima facie, amount to an offence under the Offences Against the Person Act 1861. Consent provides a defence only if the case falls into one of the accepted category of exceptions. The only potentially applicable category in this case is the category of medical procedures. However, it is clear from *R v BM*[3] that bodily modification, even at the request of a patient, does not fall within this category unless it can be therapeutically justified. Such a

[1]1994] 1 AC 212.

[2][2018] EWCA Crim 560.

[3][2018] EWCA Crim 560.

justification seems very unlikely in this case. It should be emphasised that it is Sarah, not Ian, who will be guilty of the offence.[4]

5.2.2 *Jonathan Herring (JH)*

As the Court of Appeal noted in *BM*, the issues in this kind of case raise a variety of concerns. Some concerns are real, but do not constitute insurmountable objections to the legality of such practices. Such concerns would include concerns about the sterility of the surgical environment, about effective consent, and about the surgery resulting in a burden on the NHS. While these may be legitimate concerns under the current system of regulation, they can all be addressed fairly easily under another regime of regulation and enforcement.

Another concern which might be raised is the impact on the autonomy of others: we discuss this in Scenario 2. Unlike that scenario (breast enlargement), it is unlikely that many people will feel pressurised into following Ian's example. But there may be concern that the lupine modification may truncate Ian's own autonomy later in life—if he changes his mind about the desirability of the changes. In other words there is a clash between respect for current autonomy and respect for future autonomy. This kind of argument is commonly raised in relation to children.

I would rather put this argument in terms of being open to change and to new directions. A core part of thriving is the willingness and ability to learn, change and adapt. A life in which one follows a particular set of hobbies or attitudes until they become humdrum is a limited one. A life which is open to new experiences, new ways of looking at the world, and new relationships is a thriving one. A decision which restricts one's ability to change and respond to new inputs is a limited one. If, therefore, surgery impacts on the ability to grow and develop as a person, it will undermine thriving.

The concern then becomes one about human dignity or decency. Is there something about the nature of humans and the specialness of the human body which is infringed by the procedure? I wonder too whether there might be concern about the dignity of wolves? Is it demeaning to wolves for a human to pretend they can adopt their appearance? There may be a concern similar to the concept of cultural appropriation where a person from one culture seeks to use the culture of another, without sensitivity, respect or understanding.

[4]The issue is not beyond doubt, but the principle in *R v Tyrell* [1894] 17 Cox CC 716, that a victim cannot be charged as an accomplice to a crime against them probably governs this scenario. See further J. Herring, 'Victims as defendants' in A Reed and M Bohlander, *Participation in Crime* (2013, Routledge).

5.2.3 Charles Foster (CF)

Darwin taught us, 150 years ago, that the boundaries between species are porous. But this does not mean that the notion of a species is meaningless. Far from it. Humans are importantly different from non-humans. Ian is a human, and can only thrive as a human. It is true that humans are highly adaptable creatures. And as JH says, a 'core part of thriving is the willingness and ability to learn, change and adapt'. But there are limits. Those limits are imposed by our biology and psychology. A human who wanted to be a cow, and therefore ate nothing but grass, would die. His wasting and death could not be described as thriving. Nor can Ian's surgery be described as human thriving—and Ian, being human, can know no other kind of thriving. There is nothing normatively human about his surgery. He is cutting himself off from the human community, and it is only in human community that humans can thrive.

It is dangerously unfashionable to talk about 'normative' human characteristics. I yield to no one in my defence of human self-determination, but that defence sometimes involves defending self-determination against itself: self-determination can result in the destruction of the self. One can see this in some individuals who are so self-centred that they have ceased to be anything other than their own conceits. Human conceits are always less substantial than real humans. The self that is the subject of legitimate human self-determination will always be a *human* self.

Just as it is hard, when one examines them over the evolutionary millennia, to delineate the boundaries between species, so it is hard to delineate exactly the boundaries of normality and pathology. But that does not mean that it is meaningless to talk about normality and pathology. Some behaviour is plainly within the bell curve; some towards the tails of the curve; and some outside the bounds of even the most generously drawn curve. For my part, I would gladly accept that many traits commonly stigmatized as psychiatric should be regarded (and celebrated) as variants of normal. But Ian's behaviour cannot, and to pretend that it can risks a repercussive redefinition of 'human'. Such a redefinition is objectionable not primarily because it offends against some abstract conception of human dignity (although it does, and the language of dignity is useful shorthand in such debates as this) but because it misleads us into thinking that there is an unlimited number of ways in which humans can have satisfactory lives: that is simply, as a matter of biological and sociological fact, untrue. It is no kindness to Ian, or to the others who might be influenced by his example, to pretend otherwise.

This answers the ethical question: 'Should Sarah perform the operation?' It does not follow that the law should prohibit her from doing so. The law should hesitate long before intervening: compulsion is intrinsically offensive. But here law and ethics should speak with one voice: there should be a criminal sanction.[5]

[5]For discussion of the question of whether it is right to prosecute the operator and not the customer, see http://blog.practicalethics.ox.ac.uk/2018/04/tongue-splitting-nipple-excision-and-ear-removal-why-prosecute-the-operator-but-not-the-customer/.

5.3 Scenario 2: Breast Enlargement

The Government has been alerted by schools and concerned parents that there is a growing craze for boyfriends to buy their girlfriends breast enlargements as an 18th birthday present. This craze has been fuelled by a television series, popular among teenagers, which is seen by some to send a message that breast enlargements increase attractiveness and are normal, or even required. Some schools report that a majority of girls in their sixth form now have breast enlargements.

5.3.1 The Law

While the decision in *R v BM*[6] might be thought to cast doubt on the legality of breast enlargement and other forms of cosmetic surgery, it is hard to believe that *BM* was intended to criminalise such a common practice. It might be claimed that there is a distinction between 'enlargement' and 'modification', although it is hard to see where the line would be drawn. Perhaps a better argument is based on paragraph 40 of the judgment in *BM:*

> Whilst the exceptions are incapable of being accommodated within any universally stated test, there are two features which may be thought to underpin almost all of them. First, they may produce discernible social benefit. That is true of the sporting exceptions and may even be true of boxing or 'dangerous exhibitions' as entertainment. It is possible that those with a religious hue might also be considered as conferring a social benefit, at least at the time they were recognised. But the second is that it would simply be regarded as unreasonable for the common law to criminalise the activity if engaged in with consent by (on behalf of) the injured party. That would apply to tattooing and piercing and, again, perhaps to those with a religious hue, including ritual male circumcision.

So it may simply be that breast enlargement is not unlawful because it is publicly acceptable, rather than by operation of some grand jurisprudential principle exempting it from criminal liability.

The only other legal question that remains is whether the girls are providing effective consent. Under the Mental Capacity Act 2005, section 3, a person can provide consent if they are able:

(a) to understand the information relevant to the decision,
(b) to retain that information,
(c) to use or weigh that information as part of the process of making the decision, or
(d) to communicate [the] decision (whether by talking, using sign language or any other means).

In our scenario, although the girls may be acting under peer pressure, and even pressure from their boyfriends, it is unlikely that the courts would find the pressure

---

[6] [2018] EWCA Crim 560.

to be such that they are unable to weigh up the information for themselves.[7] In *A Local Authority v Mrs A and Mr A* [2010] EWHC 1549 (Fam) pressure was found to have vitiated consent where a husband dominated his wife in all areas of life. She stopped contraception: the only reason she could give for stopping was that that was what her husband wanted. The facts of our case seem a long way from that.

5.3.2 JH

I would highlight two issues. The first is that the issue of autonomy is typically imagined in a highly individualised way. It is commonly claimed that 'We must be free to live our lives as we wish—provided that we do not harm others'. Yet this imagines our lives in an entirely self-absorbed, artificially sealed way. Our decisions inevitably impact on others. My autonomy interacts with and is dependent on the autonomy of others. I rely on others to exercise their autonomy to fulfil their responsibilities towards me, and others rely on me to exercise my autonomy to fulfil my responsibilities towards them. Virtually every decision I make has an impact on how others can exercise their autonomy. And that is a good thing. But it means that one should not simply say: 'I can decide what I want to do with my body'. This case shows that the decision by someone to have surgery, such as breast enlargement, has an impact on others. Indeed, looking at the issue in terms of autonomy fails to provide a solution to the dilemma.

If we take it that there is a group of young woman (group A) who are fully autonomously choosing to have this surgery, and another group (group B) who are not, we are in a position of conflict between the autonomy of each group. Either we respect the autonomy of group A and allow the surgery (even though that will interfere with the autonomy of group B), or we prohibit the surgery, which will protect the autonomy of group B - and interfere with the autonomy of group A.

Clearly more than autonomy is needed to identify the correct legal intervention in a situation of this kind. The thriving approach offers us a way to resolve the dilemma. We might say that group B (who will have their breasts enlarged without their full consent) are going to have their thriving seriously impeded. While either group may, depending on the legal response, have their autonomy rights interfered with, it is only the members of group B who are in danger of having their bodily integrity interfered with. As Jesse Wall and I have argued, the right of bodily integrity deserves greater protection than a mere autonomy right:

> If our bodies are the site or location of our subjectivity, and if our subjectivity is the basis of the moral duties that are owed to us, then it follows that our ability to use and control our own bodies is a moral and legal right. The same cannot be said for autonomy. We do not have a right to act autonomously. Rather, the autonomy of each person is a morally relevant

[7][2018] EWHC 308 (Fam).

property that requires consideration in all instances of moral deliberation. The principle of autonomy provides an overarching value that informs a range of rights and duties in relation to a range of legal issues. The principle of bodily autonomy is just one instance of this moral value informing common law rights.

In simpler terms, it is far worse to have your body touched without your consent than to have your body not touched as you would like. Having a nose piercing without your consent is worse than wanting a nose piercing but not being able to find someone who will do it.

We might also look at the role of the surgery in terms of creating a culture of wider social good. Here an argument may easily be made that breast enlargement surgery perpetuates a particular attitude towards women—an attitude reflected in pornography—one that reduces women to certain (sexual) body parts, or reinforces social messages which create high levels of body image concerns among young women. This might be contrasted with other forms of cosmetic surgery, such as pinning back ears, where there is far less tying in with other social forces which undermine a thriving environment.

5.3.3 CF

Nothing we have said in this book suggests that we do not consider self-determination to be important, or that all relationships are good. Autonomy is a crucial principle, and many relationships abusively truncate autonomy. Coercion is terrible. A relationship between a man and a woman in which the man says or implies that a woman should undergo unnecessary surgery for his gratification is abusive. The man's request results from a number of misunderstandings about human thriving. He has failed to understand that a good relationship (which is in the best interests of *both* parties to the relationship) will not depend on how either party looks (up to a point, of course: if one party has been surgically modified to look like a wolf, that might have an effect). He has failed to understand that a good relationship will entail caring and the celebration of vulnerability and variety. A massive variety of breast appearances should be celebrated, and if the woman, for whatever reason, feels embarrassed about her breasts, that embarrassment should generate tenderness in her partner, not a suggestion that she goes under the knife. He has failed to realize that, being a social animal, everything that he or his partner does or says necessarily affects others, and that, governed by a law of reciprocity that can be either beatific or diabolical, the effect on others bounces back and affects him and his partner. He has failed to understand the complexity of human beings: he appears to see his partner as mainly a breast-bearer. That attitude means that he will treat neither her nor himself in a way conducive to their thriving.

The man's attitude is therefore ethically unacceptable. But should the surgery be banned? Suppose the young woman comes to a surgeon and says that she wants the surgery because her boyfriend has asked her to get it. The surgeon should be very reluctant to agree. He should enquire specifically about whether her consent is real, or whether she has been coerced to such a degree that she cannot be said to have consented properly. He should give stern warnings about the possibility that in future she might have second thoughts about the wisdom of the procedure. And so on. And if she is under 18 he should, given her account of the reasons for the surgery, conclude that it is not in her best interests to have the surgery. (If necessary, s. 8 of the Family Law Reform Act should be amended to make it clear that there is not a presumption that a 16 or 17 year old can validly consent to surgery of this sort, because it is not really treatment). But if she is over 18, and her consent is real (even though it is consent for objectively bad reasons to a procedure that is objectively contrary to her interests), the law should not prohibit the surgery.

5.4 Scenario 3: Permanent Vegetative State

Sabina is in a permanent vegetative state. Her parents, sister and nephews and nieces visit her nearly every day. Although the medical professionals insist that there is no brain activity, the relatives enjoy singing to Sabina and telling her their news. They insist that 'somehow' Sabina is able to relate to what they are doing. The medical team wish to withdraw the nasogastric feeding that is keeping Sabina alive. The family strongly object to the withdrawal.

5.4.1 The Law

As Sabina lacks mental capacity the decision will be made, under the Mental Capacity Act 2005, on the basis of what is in her best interests. However, the courts have made it very clear, most recently in *Alder Hay v Evans,*[8] that the court can authorise treatment if it is in the best interests of the patient, but cannot require particular doctors to provide it if those doctors do not consider that they should. If the doctors have determined that it is not in Sabina's best interests to receive the treatment (which is perfectly plausible: see *Airedale NHS Trust v Bland*[9]) then they cannot be required to continue to facilitate the nasogastric feeding. If the court were to determine that it was in Sabina's best interests to receive the treatment, it seems the most they could do is order the Trust to seek another hospital which was willing to provide the treatment.

[8]Supra.

[9]Supra.

5.4.2 JH

As we have argued elsewhere, our relationships are key to our identity. In *Identity, Personhood and the Law* (2017) we wrote:

> The human self is profoundly relational. People are in their nature interdependent and vulnerable. It follows from this that the basic moral value of humans is not found in their individual capability or in their membership of the species, but rather in their relationships. …We can say that X and Y are people if their relationship reveals the moral qualities that we look for in human relationships. But we cannot imagine an isolated person, and assess their capabilities, since such a person does not exist.[10]

It follows from this that in our scenario Sabina and her family are engaging in some form of relationship and that this is a relationship which is of value and which contributes to human thriving. I accept that some will say this is a 'one sided relationship' and so cannot constitute something of moral value. My response to such an argument is twofold.

First, it overlooks the importance of seeing a relationship in its complete context. A relationship is an ongoing thing that draws meaning from what has happened in the past and from what will happen in the future. It cannot be measured, understood or appreciated by looking at a particular moment in time. We need therefore to look at the current care in the context of the previous relationship between Sabina and her family.

Second, it is false to imagine that relationships are constituted only by intellectual and rational thought. Relationships can be by touch, being together and communing. Indeed often the richest moments in a relationship are not about rational interchanges, but about sitting companionably together, or engaging in sexual activity or a hug. These are, literally, beyond words. Yet their value is intense. So we can see value and meaning in the interchange between Sabina and family even if it is hard to audit rationally. It is intensely *human* care.

5.4.3 CF

It is not really *treatment.*I agree with what JH says here, but have some further comments.

Acknowledgment that Sabina is involved in some significant relationships, notwithstanding her inability to appreciate anything about those relationships, should not lead us into vitalism. We have significant relationships with the dead, and there is a moral and legal mandate to treat dead bodies with respect, and (in some cases, such as wills) to respect the wishes of the dead. But that does not mean that we should treat the dead as we treat the living. Similarly, Sabina's PVS plainly has some ethical consequences and arguably should have some legal

[10]See Chap. 2, Sect. 2.1.

consequences. If the diagnosis of PVS is correct, and if our current understanding of PVS is correct (both very big assumptions:the diagnosis of PVS is hard, prognosis in PVS is unreliable, and the nature of the life of a patient in PVS is mysterious), then Sabina has not and never will have any sensation or awareness, good or bad. The characteristics that make her Sabina exist wholly in the eyes of other beholders. And although I contend that there is a sense in which it can be said that Sabina is still thriving, I cannot pretend, given the web of relationships in which she lives, that she is thriving as much as she did before she was in her vegetative state. Importantly this is not a question of *worth.* It cannot be said that Sabina's life is worth less than that of another. But it can be said that there is less *eudaemonia* in it than that of many others. Since her best interests consist in the relationships others have with her, it is legitimate to take those relationships into account in deciding on future action. Her closest relatives—those who spend their days and nights by her bedside—might eventually decide, as many relatives of PVS patients do, that the 'real' Sabina is dead, and that her continued biological existence is not necessary for their continued relationship with her, or even decide that her continued existence inhibits that relationship. It *may* then be the case, *on the grounds of Sabina's own best interests,* that the life-sustaining food and fluids should be withdrawn.

This is, of course, problematic. It would appear to give relatives the power to sign a warrant of execution, and, if this analysis were reflected in the law, it would not nudge society in the desirable direction of favouring altruism and caring. But there is no way round it. One cannot force somebody to have a relationship, or to feel something about a relationship. And if, as we have done, we have argued that thriving is woven primarily from relationship, we cannot complain when the argument gives us an answer we might have wanted to avoid. We need to remember, too, that it is not the relatives who kill a patient by making a decision about the withdrawal of food and fluids. It is, at least in ethics (though not in law: see *Bland)* the medical condition or accident that produced the vegetative state. That Sabina is alive at all is a result of modern medical cleverness, and the philosophical and legal agonies are creatures of that cleverness.

There is a tremendously important caveat: Permanent Vegetative State means that the patient is unconscious. Methods of diagnosing PVS (and hence coming to conclusions about prognosis) all look at consciousness. But we have argued that our consciousness may make a relatively small contribution to our identities, our preferences, our motives, our pleasures, and, more broadly, to our thriving. We are getting quite good at seeing the signs of consciousness, but we really have no idea of how to assess what our subconscious is doing. It may therefore be that to withdraw life-sustaining treatment from a patient in PVS is to interfere very significantly with their own thriving. And it is therefore strongly arguable that the precautionary principle should, for the moment, dictate an essentially vitalist approach to PVS cases.

Another important caveat relates to the elephant that stands in every consultation room and every ward. Sabina's continued biological existence is a consequence of medical care (feeding by a nasogastric tube, and antibiotic treatment for the infections she no doubt gets regularly). Her care, in a publicly funded health system, means that others will be denied care. If her continued survival is ethically and/or legally mandated because she is thriving, the thriving interests of those others will be compromised. The compromised interests of those others (with whom Sabina is in a relationship - a relationship which is a factor in her own thriving, on our hypothesis) will itself affect Sabina's thriving.

5.5 Scenario 4: Dementia

Francesca was a world- famous theoretical physicist. She has developed advanced dementia. She has recently taking to swimming nude at her local beach, singing bawdy songs at night, and giving her friends inedible cakes as presents. While none of this is particularly bothering anyone outside the family, the family are very embarrassed and believe that Fancesca would be horrified if she realised how she was behaving. They ask for a court order to place her in a local nursing home, to protect her from herself.

5.5.1 The Law

The application would come before the Court of Protection and be dealt with under the Mental Capacity Act 2005. Presuming Francesca is found to lack capacity, the court would need to assess her best interests. Under sub-section 4(6) the judge must consider

(a) the person's past and present wishes and feelings (and, in particular, any relevant written statement made by [her] when [s]he had capacity),
(b) the beliefs and values that would be likely to influence [her] decision if [s]he had capacity, and
(c) the other factors that [s]he would be likely to consider if [s]he were able to do so.

The judge should consider the family's views as to what 'would be in the person's best interests and, in particular, as to the matters mentioned in subsection (6).' The family's views, insofar as they reflected their own interests, as opposed to Francesca's interests, would be irrelevant.

The case may come down to a weighing up of Francesca's current views (she seems to be enjoying her new found hobbies) against her past views (she would, when she had capacity, have regarded the behaviour as embarrassing).

5.5.2 JH

The law under the Mental Capacity Act, and the traditional doctrine of autonomy, enshrined in the Act, give particular weight to rational decisions. But there are other important aspects of our humanity beyond the reach of rationality: there are values, feelings, emotions and intuitions. Those without capacity may have lost the power of rational thought, but that does not mean they have lost the ability to feel, care or value. There is a real danger that we elevate reasoning over other ways of interpreting and responding to the world.[11] A failure to value our non-rational humanity can lead to an assumption that the incompetent person has 'nothing to tell us'. We need to pay much more attention to the lived experiences of those lacking capacity and learn to appreciate and respect their views, emotions and humanity.

In our case, the uninhibited joy that Francesca has found in her naturism, singing and baking should not be discounted from the best interests determination on the basis that it is not the product of rational thought. Indeed it is at least rare, and perhaps impossible, for real joy to be produced by the rational mind. Joy comes to us from outside. We are suddenly overwhelmed by the love of another. We are awestruck by natural beauty. These are the richest gifts life has to offer, and clear examples of thriving, yet they are not the product of capacitous thought. Our response to this scenario should be: 'lucky Francesca'. Our rationality should not hold us back from celebrating and valuing the happiness she has found.

5.5.3 CF

I agree with JH, and have only one comment. It relates to identity—a subject discussed at length by me and JH elsewhere (Foster and Herring 2017). It is arguable that the dementia has caused Francesca to cease to exist, and for another being, related to Francesca only by the fact that it happens to occupy a body composed of some of the same cells as Francesca's, to come into being. It might be suggested that the relevant question in deciding what is in the best interests of whoever it is who goes skinny-dipping is: 'What would Francesca think would be in Francesca's interests?' But if Francesca has effectively died, this is either an irrelevant question or (at least) a question the answer to which should not be determinative of the skinny-dipper's interests. The question 'Who or what is the skinny-dipper?' is a profound and mysterious one. But it need not be answered fully in order to decide what to do about the skinny-dipper. *Whoever* she is, she is plainly thriving. If Francesca had made an advance directive indicating that in the event of her succumbing to dementia, all life-sustaining treatment should be withheld, that advance directive should have no application to the skinny-dipper. Should the skinny-dipper get a life-endangering chest infection, she should get antibiotics so that she can continue to swim, sing, and bake bad cakes.

[11] *Ibid.*

5.6 Scenario 5: Should Sperm Be Extracted?

Sami is 26. He has severe cognitive impairment following a road traffic accident. His wife, Tina, whom he married before the accident, has always wanted to have a child, and wishes Sami's doctors to extract some of Sami's sperm for her to use in assisted reproductive treatment. Tina is Sami's full time carer. She seeks a court order entitling her to remove and use the sperm.

5.6.1 The Law

This case would be dealt with in line with the principles in the Mental Capacity Act 2005, as already set out. The difficulty is that it is difficult to see, on a traditional analysis, how the removal of the sperm can be said to be in Sami's best interests. It would clearly benefit Tina, but unless Tina can show that having the child will benefit *Sami* the order will not be made. It may indeed be plausibly argued that having a child might harm Sami, because it will mean that Tina has less time to care for him.

5.6.2 JH

The traditional legal response to scenarios such as this is based on an assumption that our bodies are our own and we should have control over what happens to them. As Sami has not consented to the removal of the sperm, the removal is unlawful, unless it can be shown that it is in Sami's best interests. However, this vision of our bodies as controlled and ordered has been challenged. Chau and I have written:

> Our bodies are 'leaky', to use the term coined by Margrit Shildrick.[132] Not just in the sense that our bodies leak out material, but that the meaning and understanding of the self is a concept that cannot be fully captured by a single concept or approach. We have sought to argue that a key component of understanding our bodies is that they exist in relationship with other bodies, are inter-dependent with other bodies and are in a constant state of flux. These aspects are not caught by the approaches normally taken to legal status of bodies based on property or rights to integrity or privacy.[12]

As these arguments imply, the statement 'my body is mine' overlooks the deep inter-relatedness of our bodies and their dependence on the environment. Our bodies are giving to and taking from other bodies, and to and from the world around us, all the time. This is not to say that there does not need to be careful regulation of

[12]My Body, Your Body our Bodies.

what can be done with bodies, but it needs to be done within a relational understanding of their nature. In this case Sami's donation of the sperm may be part of the on-going relationship with Tina. In the light of the history of their relationship and what we foresee will be the future of their relationship, the removal of sperm seems a fair part of the give and take of the relationship. It opens up new ways for their relationship to thrive.

5.6.3 CF

I agree. The removal of the sperm facilitates and promotes relationship—and hence the thriving both of Sami and Tina. It emphasizes the porosity of our individual boundaries.

5.7 Scenario 6: A Dispute About Education

Katy and Lisa have two daughters. Katy is a fan of state education, and although the local state school has received bad OFSTED reports and there are newspaper reports of bullying and drug use at the school, she believes it is important for her children to have a normal upbringing. Lisa is a fan of private education. The local independent school has excellent exam results and offers a wide range of extra-curricular activities. It is known for having a strong religious ethos which it seeks to instil in its pupils. Katy and Lisa cannot resolve the disagreement and so seek a court order.

5.7.1 The Law

The case would be heard as an application for a specific issue order under the Children Act 1989. The case would be govererned by the welfare principle in section 1:

(1) *When a court determines any question with respect to—*

  (a) *the upbringing of a child; or*
  (b) *the administration of a child's property or the application of any income arising from it,*
  the child's welfare shall be the court's paramount consideration.

However, notoriously, the legislation does little to expand on the meaning or application of the welfare principle.

5.7.2 *JH*

In *Re M* Sir James Munby explained that 'a child's welfare is to be judged today by the standards of reasonable men and women in 2017, not by the standards of their parents, grandparents or great-grand parents in 1989, 1971, 1925 or 1902.' This means that judges, in applying the welfare principle, should give effect to their views of the reasonable parent, not their own views. Munby LJ explained in *Re G*[13] that:

> If the reasonable man or woman is receptive to change he or she is also broadminded, tolerant, easy-going and slow to condemn. We live, or strive to live, in a tolerant society increasingly alive to the need to guard against the tyranny which majority opinion may impose on those who, for whatever reason, comprise a small, weak, unpopular or voiceless minority. Equality under the law, human rights and the protection of minorities, particularly small minorities, have to be more than what Brennan J in the High Court of Australia once memorably described as 'the incantations of legal rhetoric'.

In *Re M* he explained that:

> the function of the judge in a case like this is to act as the 'judicial reasonable parent,' judging the child's welfare by the standards of reasonable men and women today, 2017, having regard to the ever changing nature of our world including, crucially for present purposes, ***changes in social attitudes***, and always remembering that the reasonable man or woman is receptive to change, broadminded, tolerant, easy-going and slow to condemn. We live, or strive to live, in a tolerant society. We live in a democratic society subject to the rule of law. We live in a society whose law requires people to be treated equally and where their human rights are respected. We live in a plural society, in which the family takes many forms, some of which would have been thought inconceivable well within living memory.

He went on in *Re G* to highlight three particular factors:

> First, we must recognise that equality of opportunity is a fundamental value of our society: equality as between different communities, social groupings and creeds, and equality as between men and women, boys and girls. Secondly, we foster, encourage and facilitate aspiration: both aspiration as a virtue in itself and, to the extent that it is practical and reasonable, the child's own aspirations … Thirdly, our objective must be to bring the child to adulthood in such a way that the child is best equipped both to decide what kind of life they want to lead – what kind of person they want to be – and to give effect so far as practicable to their aspirations. Put shortly, our objective must be to maximise the child's opportunities in every sphere of life as they enter adulthood.

I think these are the right questions to be asking, but would clarify three points. First, in considering aspiration, we must not be limited to educational achievement. Educational achievement might help a child achieve goods in life, but there is far more to thriving than being well-educated. The Senior Common Rooms of leading universities are not where one would expect to find well-balanced, happy, flourishing lives. Indeed given the rates of self-harm and low esteem at some of the schools with the highest educational achievements one might, on thriving grounds, be wary of a school precisely because it is high-flying. Second, throughout this

[13] [34].

book (and elsewhere) we have emphasised the importance of relationships. Which school will best set up the child to engage in a wide range of relationships? Third, we have emphasized the importance of being open to change, wonder, surprise, and joy. Which educational establishment will promote these best? Clearly we need more information to answer these questions, but they are the ones to ask.

5.7.3 CF

Again I agree. Which of the options will maximize the thriving of each of the daughters is an empirical question. One school might be best for one; the other for the other.

5.8 Scenario 7: Assisting Suicide

Xavier has been diagnosed with severe depression. He has decided that his life is not worth living, and announces to all who will listen that he would like to die. He cannot screw up the courage to kill himself and looks for someone to help him. His friend, Timothy, is sympathetic, and willing to help, but fears prosecution. Timothy seeks a direction from the court that he will not be prosecuted if he helps Xavier to commit suicide.

5.8.1 The Law

Timothy is right to be concerned. Section 2(1) of the Suicide Act 1961 (as amended) states:
A person ('D') commits an offence if—

(a) *D does an act capable of encouraging or assisting the suicide or attempted suicide of another person, and*
(b) *D's act was intended to encourage or assist suicide or an attempt at suicide.*

However the Crown Prosecution Service[14] has issued guidance on when potential defendants will be prosecuted. t. The guidance lists factors in favour of and against prosecution. In this case there might well be questions over whether the following factors in favour of prosecution apply:

[14]CPS Suicide: Policy for Prosecutors in Respect of Cases of Encouraging or Assisting Suicide (2014).

- *the victim did not have the capacity (as defined by the Mental Capacity Act 2005) to reach an informed decision to commit suicide;*
- *the victim had not reached a voluntary, clear, settled and informed decision to commit suicide.*

Although this factor against prosecution will apply:

- *the suspect was wholly motivated by compassion.*

In any event the court does not appear to have the authority to authorise in advance assistance in suicide. So Timothy's application would be unlikely to succeed.

5.8.2 JH

The issue of assisted dying has become one of the issues of the age. Yet it has attracted far too much attention. While we debate the rights and wrongs of assisted dying, older people are dying in poverty, freezing temperatures, and desperate hunger. So many are neglected by their communities, abandoned by their families, living isolated, socially excluded lives. Many spend their last months or, if they are unlucky, years, in care homes marked by abuse, neglect and over-medication. Recently it seems that barely a month goes by without stories of horrific abuse in our institutional settings for the old. But far more common than physical abuse is a setting of utter boredom, with minimal personal interaction. No love. No tenderness. No hope.

Against this background we dare to discuss the right to die? Are those supporting a right to die not concerned at the misery facing so many of our older people which will lead them to request death? Are those opposing a right to die aware of what we are otherwise leaving older people to face? I am saddened at the amount of time, intellectual energy, and political pressure taken up with the issue, when the far more important issues of trying to improve the lot of older people, improving the quality of palliative care, and combating the prevalent ageist attitudes in society are neglected. These are the issues that should generate books, marches, and internet petitions. Given the way we treat older people, those with mental health issues, and the disabled, those who trumpet either the sanctity of life or a right to die should be blushing.

For Xavier our response must be: 'I am so sorry you feel so bad you want to die. What can we do to make you feel better?' The fact that so many people would respond to this scenario with a reference to a right to die or a right to autonomy is a sad reflection of skewed priorities.

5.8.3 CF

Again I agree. It is true that simple invocation of principles such as autonomy or the 'right to life' cannot do justice to any real human situations—let alone a situation as complex as this. Only a holistic assessment of thriving can deliver a sufficiently nuanced result. Xavier may be capacitous at the times that he indicates he wishes to die, or he may not. But although this book has been primarily concerned with incapacitous adults or children, the idea of thriving should apply to all *ethical* determinations in relation to humans. As I said above, in the discussion about breast augmentation, thriving should not necessarily generate the *legal* answer. If Xavier is incapacitous at the material time, then could a properly conducted best interests determination conclude that it is in his best interests to die? This will be a highly fact-sensitive question. It will depend on the results of an audit of the medical options for treatment of the condition that makes his life wretched, and of the options for his future day-to-day life. If it is the case that it is in his best interests to die then, as JH implies, it is an indictment of the thriving of *everyone* in the society in which Xavier lives: we would all, as John Donne said, be diminished.[15]

One might or might not think that Timothy's desire to help Xavier is misconceived, but whatever one says about him, he is a man who takes his friendships seriously. He is prepared to shoulder an onerous burden. He acknowledges that he and Xavier are bound intimately together. In Xavier's isolation, the fact of that solidarity with Timothy must be a comfort: it must help him to thrive; it must humanize Xavier even at the point when he is most tempted to leave the human race. My own view is that the assisted suicide legislation serves a crucial purpose, but whatever one's views about that, perhaps it can be agreed that at least in many cases the CPS guidelines steer a skilled and humane course between the need to assert the preciousness of life and the need not to penalize compassionate solidarity with the desperate.

Reference

Foster C, Herring J (2017) Identity, Personhood and the Law. Springer, London

[15]'Any man's death diminishes me/ Because I am involved in mankind/And therefore never send to know for whom the bell tolls/ It tolls for thee.' 'No man is an island'.

Chapter 6
Conclusion

We began this book by demonstrating (in Chap. 1) that the law is rarely explicit about what account of human thriving it adopts when making best interests determinations. That judges must be making *some* assumptions about what is entailed by a Good Life is obvious. It is plainly desirable, for many reasons, that those assumptions are made explicit. The assumptions can sometimes be read between the lines of the judgments: we have tried to do so.

The account adopted should take cognizance of the views about the nature of man and hence the nature of human thriving that have evolved over the millennia: we surveyed those views in Chaps. 2 and 3. And it should also take account of the evidence that has emerged about what, as a matter of fact, makes humans happy. We surveyed that evidence in Chap. 4. There is more to thriving than mere jollity or contentment, but deep, abiding happiness is, or approaches, the *eudaemonia* that Arisotle identified as the hallmark of the Good Life. We saw that there is a remarkable concordance between the views of the ancient human traditions about the Good Life and the findings of modern science about the elements of happiness, and an even more remarkable discordance between the evidence and the ancients, and the principles applied by the judges (when we can discern them). The difference turns on a view of the nature of the human person: until the Renaissance, humans were seen (as the science indicates that they are) as highly social, relational creatures, with concomitant duties and expectations. Thereafter they were increasingly seen as discrete islands. This unbiological view has been adopted by the courts, who make decisions on the basis of a simplistic pastiche of the highly complex, interrelational animals that humans really are. Good ethics, it is said, demand good facts. So does good law. It is time that the law got the facts right about the humans whose thriving is its only legitimate objective.

C. Foster and J. Herring, *Human Thriving and the Law*, SpringerBriefs in Law,
https://doi.org/10.1007/978-3-030-01135-2_6

MIX
Papier aus verantwortungsvollen Quellen
Paper from responsible sources
FSC® C105338

If you have any concerns about our products,
you can contact us on
ProductSafety@springernature.com

In case Publisher is established outside the EU,
the EU authorized representative is:
Springer Nature Customer Service Center GmbH
Europaplatz 3, 69115 Heidelberg, Germany

Printed by Libri Plureos GmbH
in Hamburg, Germany